The HEART of Christmas

The HEART of Christmas

Max Lucado
John Maxwell
Jack Hayford
Bill Hybels
David Jeremiah
Rick Warren

THOMAS NELSON PUBLISHERS
Nashville

Published in Nashville, Tennessee, by Thomas Nelson, Inc.

ISBN 0-7852-8213-0 (hardcover)

Printed in the United States of America.

Contents

Introduction

Christmas, for most of us, is a time of festive celebration. It is an occasion for renewing precious friendships. It is an opportunity to reminisce about days gone by. It's a great excuse to eat too much, sing too loudly, and spend more money than we should. Christmas can stir up intense and complex feelings—both pleasurable and painful—that sometimes take us by surprise. And for Christians, Christmas is a time of awe and reverence and wonder, when the timeless story of Christ's birth is read, once again, from the Gospels for all the world to hear.

Some of the most cherished Christmas joys

are found in family traditions that link one year to another with the harmony of favorite carols, the sparkle of familiar ornaments, and the time-honored rites of gift giving. Year after year, decade after decade, we delight in seeing the same front-yard holiday decorations on the same neighborhood streets. We are thrilled at the re-appearance of well-worn downtown Christmas lights and garlands. We are cheered when the church sets up its venerable nativity scene, angels, shepherds, wise men and all.

But the very familiarity of Christmas sometimes causes us to overlook the most vital expressions of what should be a meaningful season. We have listened to the words of the great Christmas hymns so many times since childhood that we sometimes fail to appreciate their eloquent poetry. We have heard a hundred times about Mary and Joseph's long, weary trek from Nazareth to Bethlehem, but we haven't always stopped to remember just exactly how and why it happened. We've almost memorized the Bible story, we've sung the carols, we've hung the holly, and we've baked the turkey. When it comes to Christmas, we've done it all.

And yet, somewhere along the way, we may have lost touch with the heart of Christmas itself.

With that in mind, this unique and priceless collection has been titled *The Heart of Christmas* in hopes that through its message, we can once again feel the pulse and experience the energy of a miraculous story that transfuses new life into all who will truly listen. In the pages that follow, six of America's most beloved communicators share their favorite Christmas messages. Their words gently remind us of the beautiful, the inspirational, and the profoundly spiritual facets of Christmas that we may have begun to overlook. They offer life lessons we may have forgotten. They provide us with priceless faith perspectives that are sometimes eclipsed by the gleam and glitter of earthbound gifts.

Each of these communicators offers a wealth of insight, a penetrating understanding of God's Word, and an extra measure of storytelling skill.

John Maxwell asks a question that carries us far beyond the manger and the distant hills of Palestine, and leads us all the way back to our own little corner of the world: "What do you do when you follow a star and find a stable?" Yes, it happens to everybody once in a while. And as we ponder, we find inspiration, for there are some very wise and wonderful ways to deal with the "stables" in our lives. This is a message for those of us whose dreams—perhaps even Christmas dreams—have not been fulfilled, at least not in the way we'd hoped.

Bill Hybels takes us on a tour of our local nativity scene, and encourages us to look with new vision upon the familiar elements there. He suggests that we lift our eyes heavenward to the star, that we take an extra moment to gaze at the stable, and that we allow God to speak to us as we peer into the manger. In the all too familiar surrounding of the "Christmas scene" we come to a renewed understanding of God's grace, and our hearts are touched with gratitude.

Max Lucado helps us to reflect upon the life

of Jesus' adoptive father, and he invites us to walk alongside Joseph through the fields near Bethlehem. As we join the expectant father pacing beneath the stars as he awaits the imminent birth in the nearby stable, we share the thoughts and questions Joseph must have had as he found himself an eyewitness to the Messiah's miraculous arrival. Yes, Joseph wanted to be a father, but he certainly never imagined his baby being born quite like this!

David Jeremiah explores the significance of names in general, and of the Christmas baby's name in particular. He discusses the Hebrew and prophetic meanings of "salvation," and considers why God chose to call His only begotten Son "Jesus." As we read, we recall the many reasons that we treasure the name of Jesus above all other names.

Rick Warren tells us about the three greatest gifts that Christmas can offer, no matter where we celebrate Christmas, whom we share the season with, or how we choose to remember the coming of God's Son into the world. "You've celebrated every Christmas for as many years as you are old," he points out, "you know the songs and the stories, and you know what it's all about, but you've never unwrapped the gift."

Finally, in his expressive, warmhearted style, Jack Hayford reconsiders Mary, Jesus' mother, and the remarkable role she played in God's plan of redemption. We are led along with her through her astonishing encounter with the angel, through her months of preparation for childbirth, and through her growing awareness of God's unprecedented blessing on her young life. As we read, we consider anew the tremendous faith and obedience she demonstrated as she became the first to receive God's gift to the world as her own.

From the hearts of America's favorite communicators, here is the good news about the Christmas gift of a lifetime—"Christ, by highest heaven adored; Christ, the everlasting Lord!" Here is the gospel message of His loving presence. Here is the Bethlehem child's blessing, wrapped in unique and colorful words, promising hours of rereading, reflection, and returning once again to *The Heart of Christmas*.

The HEART of Christmas

"CHRISTMAS IS
ABOUT A BABY, BORN
IN A STABLE, WHO
CHANGED THE WORLD
FOREVER."
JOHN
MAXWELL

JOHN MAXWELL

When You FOLLOW A STAR AND FIND A STABLE

he actress Helen Hayes once told a story about cooking her first Thanksgiving turkey. She explained that she wasn't a very good cook, but after several years of marriage, she decided to try preparing a turkey on her own. She sat her husband and son down before the meal and said, "This may not come out exactly the way you want it to. If it's not a good turkey, don't say a thing. Without any comment, just stand up from the table, and we'll go to the nearest restaurant and eat."

A few moments later, Helen walked into the dining room with the turkey. Her husband and son were already standing with their coats and hats on!

Our expectations definitely control our conduct.

We conduct our life and our daily affairs based on what we expect from them. Kids provide a classic example. I would imagine that if you have grade school children in your house, you have no problem getting them up on Christmas morning. If you're like my wife, Margaret, and me, before you go to bed on Christmas Eve you pray, "Oh, God, let them sleep!" But the day after New Year's, when those same kids have to go back to school, it's an entirely different matter. Why? Because their conduct is controlled and influenced by their expectations.

What If You Follow a Star and Find a Stable?

In Matthew chapter 2, we read the story of the wise men following the star. And, based on that Scripture, the question that I have for you is this: What happens when you've been following a star, and it leads you to a stable? What happens when all of a sudden, after thinking that something grand and glorious would be at the other end, you end up in the backyard of a barn? And there, instead of a palace and a king on a throne, you find a little baby held by his mother. It's nothing like what you had anticipated. How do you react when you follow the star and find a stable? How is your conduct affected by the outcome of your expectations?

> Now after Jesus was born in Bethlehem of Judea in the days of Herod the king, behold, magi from the east arrived in Jerusalem, saying, "Where is He who has been born King of the Jews? For we saw His star in the east, and have come to worship Him." And when Herod the king heard it, he was troubled, and all Jerusalem with him. And gathering together all the chief priests and scribes of the people, he began to inquire of them where the Christ was to be born. And they said to him, "In Bethlehem of Judea, for so it has been written by the prophet, 'And you, Bethlehem, land of Judah, are by no means least among the leaders of Judah; for out of you shall come forth a Ruler, who will shepherd My people Israel.'" Then Herod secretly called the magi, and ascertained from them the time the star appeared. And he sent them to

> Bethlehem, and said, "Go and make careful search for the Child; and when you have found Him, report to me, that I too may come and worship Him." And having heard the king, they went their way; and lo, the star, which they had seen in the east, went on before them, until it came and stood over where the Child was. And when they saw the star, they rejoiced exceedingly with great joy. And they came into the house and saw the Child with Mary His mother; and they fell down and worshiped Him; and opening their treasures they presented to Him gifts of gold and frankincense and myrrh. And having been warned by God in a dream not to return to Herod, they departed for their own country by another way. (Matt. 2:1–12 NASB)

Can you imagine the disappointment the Magi must have felt when they finally ended up in Bethlehem? We know that they were expecting a mansion or a royal court. They even stopped at King Herod's palace to find out about this star and this child who was to be born.

Every one of us has had times in life when we've followed a star. Everything looked so promising, but we were to find out at the end that we were in a stable. Margaret's nephew Troy was a promising young athlete with a great mind. He was a good student in his second year in college. Troy was very handsome, and it seemed that he had everything at his fingertips. Then one night he was in a terrible automobile accident, thrown over one hundred feet from a car. He ended up in intensive care in a Columbus, Ohio, hospital. If you had looked at Troy just hours before his accident, you would have said, "There's a kid following a star. His future is unlimited." Afterward, we could only wonder if he had a future.

Go back to your high school graduation pictures and look at some of the kids whom you graduated with. Some of them started off with such promise. Perhaps you look at the things they wrote in your yearbook and think back—you were sure they would someday be a star. But now, as you look at them, you can see that life has been a disappointment.

College kids graduate with their diploma tucked under their arm, ready to go out and win the world. But they find out that the job they wanted is not the one that they got.

So many times I have stood before an altar and married a couple, so promising, so gorgeous. Everybody thought their marriage had tremendous possibilities, only to find out a few years later it was lying in ruin in divorce court.

Maybe it's your job, where you've been expecting a promotion. Finally the boss calls you into the office. As you sit there expectantly, you find out that you've been passed over—someone else got that position. You walk out of the office in a daze, realizing that even though you've been following a star, you ended up in a stable.

Maybe Mom and Pop are going to start a business. All their life together, they've regularly set aside a little bit of money for it. Finally the day comes when they can go down to the bank and leverage a loan, and off they go. They have such excitement as they open the doors, only to find out that they are a lot more excited than the potential customers outside on the street. They're been following a star—but one day they wake up and find themselves in a stable.

I've seen many people come to retirement age, and they can hardly wait to get away from the grind of work. All their life they've worked so hard, and they finally get their gold watch. But they find out a couple of months later that retirement isn't really what they thought it was going to be. They get restless and unsettled. What happened? Well, they thought that they were following the star, but when they got to their destination, it was a stable.

There's a message that I preach to pastors at conferences, called, "Flops, Failures, and Fumbles." It's kind of my life story. In it I describe all the stupid things I've done in the ministry. It makes other pastors feel wonderful. I especially like to preach this message at the end of a conference when all they've heard about is success. It just kind of lets them know that everybody makes mistakes. Sometimes when you follow the star, it doesn't lead you where you want to go.

I read something the other day written by a pastor who had obviously visited a few stables along the way. He said,

My counselor has finally forced me to face the fact that I'm a failure in my ministry. Permit me to list my evangelical demerits: I've never been to the Holy Land, I mean, not even as a visitor, let alone as a tour guide. I wince whenever I see those ads that say "Go to the Holy Land" in a religious magazine. My wife even stopped buying Kosher wieners because they make me feel convicted. Every program I've ever started has failed. Our evangelism explosion didn't explode; it gave an embarrassed pop and rolled over and died. I attended a Church Growth Seminar, and while I was gone six families left the church. A refugee family that we tried to sponsor refused to come—the last I heard they were seeking asylum in a Chinese restaurant in St. Louis. Whenever I try Dial-A-Prayer I get the wrong number, usually a funeral home or a chicken carry-out place. I tried to

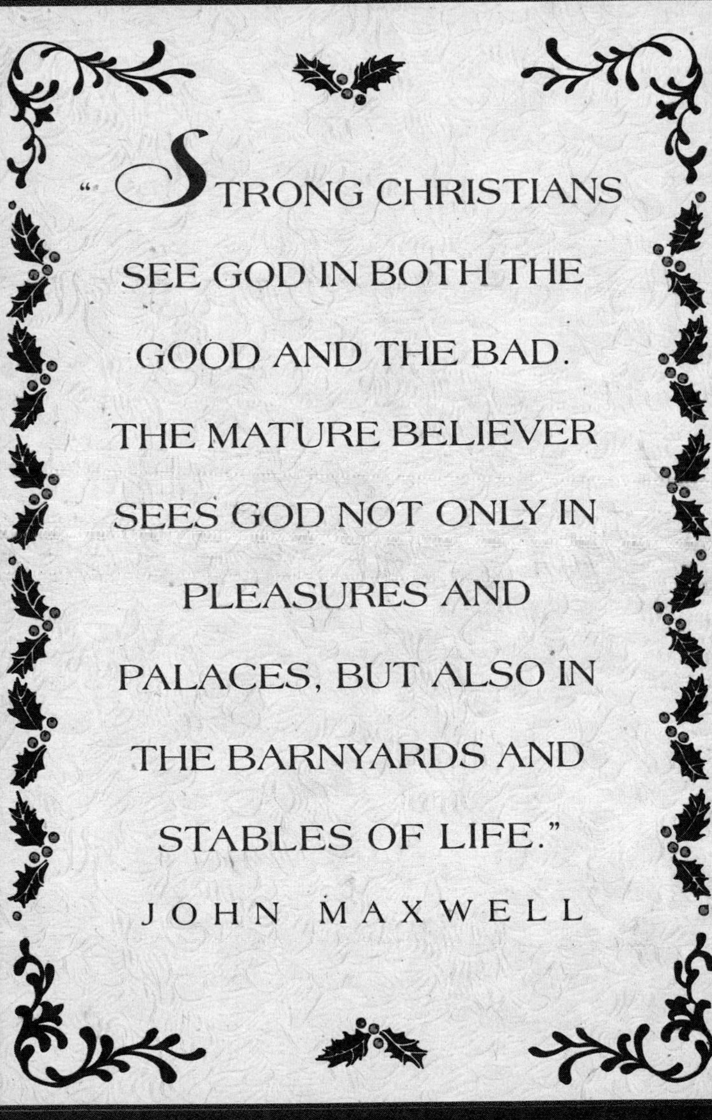
"STRONG CHRISTIANS
SEE GOD IN BOTH THE
GOOD AND THE BAD.
THE MATURE BELIEVER
SEES GOD NOT ONLY IN
PLEASURES AND
PALACES, BUT ALSO IN
THE BARNYARDS AND
STABLES OF LIFE."
JOHN MAXWELL

> Dial-A-Meditation, and the tape broke after the first sentence, which was "So things aren't going well today." Our church teams never win any games. Baseball, basketball, volleyball, shuffleboard . . . you name it, we've lost it. The town Little League champs challenged us and won. I am thinking of sharing all of this with our denominational leaders, but they're never around when I phone, and all their letters to me are addressed to occupant. I've been told that failure can be the back door to success, but the door seems to be locked and I can't find the key. Any suggestions?

That is the picture of a man who followed a star but found only a stable.

In "Peanuts," Lucy sometimes feels like being the psychiatrist. One day, she puts up her little sign: "Psychiatric Help 5¢." As usual, her first customer is Charlie Brown. But this time, she's so frustrated with him that she says, "Charlie Brown, sometimes I feel we are not communicating. You, Charlie Brown, are a foul ball in the line drive of life. You're often in the shadow of your goalpost. You're a miscue. You're three putts on the 18th green. You're a seven-ten split in the tenth frame. You are a dropped rod and reel in the lake of life. You're a missed free throw. You're a shanked nine iron. You're a called third strike. You're a bug on the windshield of life. Do you understand? Do I make myself clear?"

The beautiful part of the Christmas story of the wise men is what they do when they come to that stable. Through their actions, they teach us three things. I believe that all wise men throughout the ages have done these three things when they come upon a stable—to a place or situation that isn't exactly what they were expecting.

When Wise Men Find a Stable, They Look for *God*

Wise men of every age, when handed a difficult situation, don't panic about the problem, but hold steady and say, "God is somewhere in this stable of life. There's something I can learn. I'll hold steady because God is somewhere in this."

One of the things I like about the Bible is that the writers never try to make the Bible characters better than they really were. They just tell it like it was.

Look at Joseph, who was a very wise man. He understood how to find the good in the bad. Remember all the things that he went through? He was sold into slavery, lied to by his brothers. In a new land, in slavery, he was lied to again while working in Potiphar's house. He went through one setback after another. But finally God raised him up to be prime minister of Egypt. When his brothers came back, they apologized. What did Joseph say? He said, "You meant it for evil, but God meant it for good." Joseph had the ability to see God in the stable.

Look at Job, who found himself sitting on an ash heap. He was a good man who never did anything wrong. Yet there he was, going through persecution, loss of family, loss of fortune, friends standing around telling him to curse God and die. But Job didn't listen to their advice. Instead, he said, "The Lord gives, and the Lord takes away. Blessed be the name of the Lord." Job was able to see God in the stable of life.

Look at David, writing the Twenty-third Psalm in a cave while fleeing from his own son who wanted to take over his throne. David had the ability to follow the star, yet when he found the stable, he somehow saw God in it.

Look at the apostle Paul. Even while he was in prison, he was writing to the church at Philippi, offering an uplifting message and telling them to cheer up. When he came to a stable in his life, Paul was able to see God in it.

The difference between a weak Christian and a strong Christian is right here:

Weak Christians see God only in the good. When good things come along, the weak and immature Christian says, "Well, it must be from God, since everything good is happening." I always cringe when I hear somebody say, "Well it's just working out so well, I know God must be in it." Not necessarily.

Strong Christians see God in both the good and the bad. The mature believer sees God not only in pleasures and palaces, but also in the barnyards and stables of life.

When Margaret and I lived in Ohio, we were in the process of trying to adopt our second child. We already had Elizabeth, and we were working with a wonderful Christian agency from Oklahoma City. We'd flown out and been interviewed once. And they were excited because they thought they had a boy for us.

When they called us, I was holding a conference in southern Ohio, and Margaret and I were together in a resort area with some other pastors. With great excitement, they told us that in three or four days we would have a boy. But the next day they called again and said, "We're sorry, but the state of Ohio won't let us bring the boy in because they found out that we only allow Christian parents to adopt children. They say we are not giving equal rights." The state had interfered.

Margaret and I sat in a room by ourselves realizing that the boy we had been expecting in a couple of days would not be our boy. We literally heard that bad news fifteen minutes before I was to go out and speak to pastors again. So we cried, trusted, and said, "God, Your ways are higher than ours. We don't understand this, but that's all right." Disappointed as I was, I went out and spoke.

That was in January. Two months later, Joel Porter was born. Little did we realize that God, in His sovereignty, had already chosen the boy that we were to have, the boy that brings incredible delight to me, in all of his orneriness. His orneriness delights me because I was just like him.

In 1980 we left Lancaster, and I went to Marion, Indiana, for a year and a half to oversee evangelism for the denomination. It was the most miserable year and a half that Margaret and I have ever spent. I was traveling all the time, and she was staying home. In Lancaster, we'd left a beautiful home right next door to my brother, out in the country in the woods. We'd bought another home in Marion. In the year and a half we were there a real estate depression hit, and houses went down in price. By the time we made the shift to come to pastor Skyline, we had lost over $20,000 on our house. But think of it—if I hadn't gone to Marion, Indiana, I wouldn't have come to San Diego. When I was following a star, I came into a stable. But God was there.

Here's the point. You may be walking into a stable period in your life. You've been following that star, and it looks so good. Then all of a sudden you say, "Is this it?" Remember, wise men have the ability to see God in the stables of their lives.

When Wise Men Find a Stable, They Offer Their *Very Best* to God

Wise men also give their best when they come to a stable. But that isn't our natural inclination. You see, instead of offering gold and frankincense and myrrh in the stable of life that we didn't expect, our temptation is to hold back. In fact, when we find a stable instead of a palace, we're often tempted to refuse to give anything, much less our very best.

The marriage isn't what it should be, and all of a sudden we say, "Well maybe I want to hold back." We begin to stifle our feelings and to withdraw. When we come to a stable of life, to a time when we need to give our very best, that's when we're tempted not to offer the best we have. I think all of us need to go through what I call the "mirror test." Every day when I get up and look in the mirror, I need to ask myself, "Am I giving my very best in the situation that I'm in?" That situation may be one of many problems, or it may be one of great prosperity.

When the wise men came to the stable, they didn't withhold anything. They didn't look at one another and say, "You know, if we didn't leave anything here, we'd have this gold and frankincense for Herod. Maybe we should give it to him and his family. This is just a kid in a backyard stable. Certainly we don't need to give Him all of this expensive stuff."

The difference between the average and above average person lies in just three words: *And Then Some*. Great men of God, and great men of society, give their very best, and then some. They forgive people, and then some. They're always walking the extra mile. They're always taking the extra step. It's an effort.

Winston Churchill said, "The world is being run by tired men." He meant that those who really make a mark for God or for history cannot afford to function without sufficient energy. Those who make a difference are those who take the extra step, walk the second mile, give their very best to a situation, even when it doesn't look promising.

It's a joy to share this truth at Christmastime, because people can grab it. But sometimes average folks don't quite live up to it. A couple of years ago we took the kids to the Washington

Monument. There was a two-hour wait to get on the elevator to go to the top. In my impatience, I walked up to the guy by the elevator and asked, "Is there any way we can make it up faster?" He looked at me and said, "You can go up now, if you're willing to take the stairs." I went back to the line.

Powerful, isn't it? *"You can go up now, if you're willing to take the stairs."*

You see, the average person in life wants to ride elevators. Average people want to get by doing the least, not the best. They're always saying, "How can I cut a couple of hours off work and do my least?" In America, this mind-set has given us shoddiness and a haphazard workforce, which has allowed other countries to dominate and become more powerful in industry. Why? Because we lost that extra effort that brings excellence.

Whether it's in preaching, or working in a factory, or at your own business, or within your own family, the mark of a Christian is that he will walk the second mile and turn the other cheek.

A wise man or woman gives the extra effort, all for the glory of the Lord Jesus Christ.

WHEN WISE MEN FIND A STABLE, THEY *CHANGE THEIR DIRECTION*

Have you ever had a stable experience that changed your life? I've had many. In my first year at my first pastorate, I made a hospital visit to a fellow who wasn't a Christian. I never witnessed to him, and I saw him five times. I was a "nice guy." Oh, I would pray a little prayer, maybe quote a little Scripture, but I never talked to him about his soul. Then one Friday afternoon after I left him in the hospital, by the time I got to my car in the parking lot, he had died.

When I got home, my wife was on the phone talking to one of his sisters, saying, "Yes, I'm sure my husband would be glad to do the funeral."

I flippantly said, "Sure, I'll do the funeral. After all, pastors do funerals."

It wasn't until we were at the funeral home with his two sisters at my side, looking into that casket, that it hit me. I saw a man that I'd had a conversation with three days earlier, and I realized that he was lost for eternity, with no hope of salvation, forever without God, because John Maxwell did not have the spiritual power and anointing to witness in the name of Jesus Christ. It was a stable in my life.

I remember weeping with those two sisters. They were moved to see that I was moved. They thought I was weeping over the loss of a friend. But I was weeping because God was showing me myself, and the picture was not good. It was a picture of a person who walks into a stable and says, "Hey, so what?" instead of giving it his best shot, instead of looking for God. For the next six months I sought God. I sought the anointing. I was miserable. I made my wife miserable. But it was in that stable of life that my life changed direction, never to be the same again.

Besides my Bible, there are two books that have changed my life's direction. One of them is *Here I Stand* by Roland Bates. It's about the life of Martin Luther. I read it when I was twenty years of age. It was a paperback book, but I had my mother put a hardback on it to keep it intact because it changed my life. Martin Luther had the guts to stand up against all odds. He risked his life and said, "Here I stand; I can do nothing else." It changed me.

I also read *Spiritual Leadership* by Oswald Sanders. When I read about what was important in being a spiritual man of God, that changed me, too. When you've come upon the stables of life, have you ever sensed that God wanted you to change directions?

Henry David Thoreau decided to get into Walden's Pond one day and sink down until the water was at eye level, so he could see the world through the eyes of a frog. I always thought, *How stupid; and really, who cares?* But I began to think about Henry David Thoreau this week. I began to think about Christmas, and I began to think about God. Do you realize that's what God did? The God of the universe, with no limitations, allowed Himself to be born of the virgin Mary. He looked through human eyes and grew up like you and me, so that He would understand us and know how to relate to us. If Christmas is anything, Christmas is the story of God changing worlds and putting limitations upon Himself. It's the story of a baby born in Bethlehem, who was more powerful than the Roman Empire that existed that day.

Let me share something with you that I think is very important. Read carefully.

> A century ago, men were following with bated breath the march of Napoleon and waiting feverishly for news of the war. And all the while in their own homes, babies were being born. But who could think about babies? Everybody was thinking about battles. In one year, there stole into a world a host of heroes. Gladstone was born in Liverpool, England, and Tennyson at Somersby. Oliver Wendell Holmes

was born in Massachusetts. The very same day of that same year, Charles Darwin made his debut at Shrewsbury. Abraham Lincoln drew his first breath in Old Kentucky, and music was enriched by the birth of Felix Mendelssohn in Hamburg. But nobody thought about babies. Everybody was thinking about battles. Yet, which of the battles of 1809 mattered more than the babies that were born in 1809? We fancy that God can only manage His world through the big battalions of life, when all the while He is doing it through the beautiful babies that are being born into the world. When a wrong wants righting, or a truth wants preaching, or a continent wants opening, God sends a baby into the world to do it. And where do you find God on Christmas? In a manger. A baby was born at the heart of the Roman Empire, that when the Roman Empire would crumble and fall, that baby, who would become a man, would also become a Savior of the world.

When the wise men found the stable, they also found a baby. When people ask me about the future, I tell them one thing: "The greatest men of God are not world-class preachers. They aren't famous, and they aren't media idols. The greatest man of God is not the pastor of a church. The greatest man of God is a baby."

You know, we see so many babies all around us—maybe one of them is the next John Wesley. Do you realize as you gather around the Christmas tree and open presents, that one of your own little kids may be the next Billy Graham? Oh, the hands, the feet, the minds, and the souls that we have the privilege of guiding! Our children are watching us. They are seeing our Christian example, our commitment to the Lord, our faithful witness. They are storing all that away in their hearts, and someday they'll become great men and women of God.

If Christmas is about anything, it's about a baby—God's baby, born in a stable, who changed the world forever. When we come to the stables in our lives, let us be wise and remember to look for God. Let us bring Him the best we have to offer. And let us allow Him to change the direction of our lives, enabling us to become the great men and women of God He wants us to be.

"And they . . . saw the Child with Mary His mother: and they fell down and worshiped Him."

MATTHEW 2:11 NASB

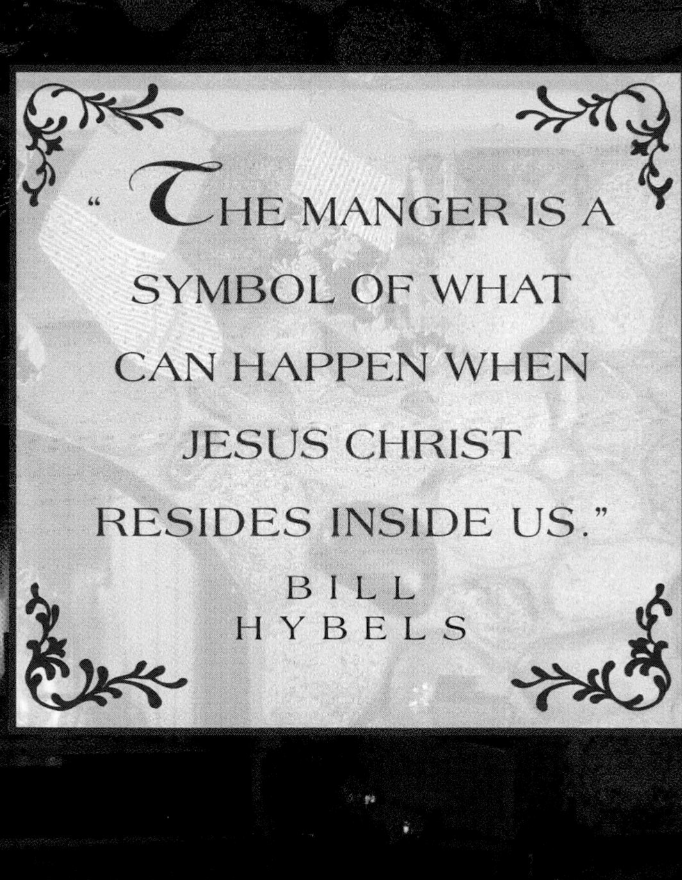
"THE MANGER IS A
SYMBOL OF WHAT
CAN HAPPEN WHEN
JESUS CHRIST
RESIDES INSIDE US."
BILL
HYBELS

BILL HYBELS

Seeing the CHRISTMAS SCENERY

ll your life you've seen nativity scenes. As you grew up you saw them in your neighborhood, on church lawns and in public squares. You've seen nativity scenes on Christmas cards and on billboards and on video monitors and on beer commercials. They're everywhere this time of year, and by now you've probably seen so many of them that they've probably started to fade into the landscape.

We've all seen nativity scenes throughout our lives. But instead of turning away in disinterest, let's spend some unrushed moments looking at them a little more carefully. Let's notice some of the particulars that make up a nativity scene, particulars that often get overlooked. For example, use your own built-in zoom lens system and focus for a moment on the star above the stable.

The *Star*—God Provides a *Travel Guide* for Seekers

Believe it or not, the Bible tells us that God commissioned a particular star to serve as a kind of travel guide for a group of men from the East who had developed an interest in looking for the Christmas child. Not only did that star lead these Easterners to Jerusalem and then to Bethlehem, but Matthew 2:9 tells us that the star led the wise men to the exact location of Joseph, Mary, and Jesus. And when they finally located Him, the Scriptures say they fell to their knees and worshiped Him and gave Him costly gifts.

The text of Scripture states clearly that the wise men rejoiced over the fact that God had provided them with a remarkably accurate travel guide. Deep down they knew they never would have found Christ without the star. The Christmas star was God's gift of direction—God's travel guide for seekers.

Look at the star this Christmas. Look at it a little differently. Look at it as a symbol of the fact that God has always provided travel guides to earnest spiritual seekers. Throughout history, God has seen to it that those who diligently seek after Christ will find Him.

Many of us are dedicated Christians. All of us who are Christians can look back to a time when we were just getting interested in spiritual realities. Remember how confused we all were? Remember how lost we felt? Remember how overwhelming it all seemed to us as we were trying to sort things out? Remember what God did?

God provided a travel guide for each of us—someone to lead us to Christ. It might have been a mom or dad. It might have been a guy at work, a neighbor, a close friend, a teacher or a pastor. But all of us who are Christians can retrace our spiritual journeys and say, "Without that person, that pastor, that teacher, that friend, I doubt I would ever have found Christ." God sent someone to cross our path. He sent someone whose light was bright. He sent someone whose love was real. He sent someone whose faith was so compelling that we found ourselves trusting that earthbound travel guide to lead us to Christ.

What would some of our lives be like—who would we be, what would we be doing?—had it not been for an earthbound star that God used as a travel guide in our lives? Isn't Christmas an appropriate time to thank God for the gift of travel guides? Why not take a minute and assign a name to the star or stars that God provided for you, to lead you from your confusion to Christ.

But perhaps you feel a whole lot more like someone who is still seeking than someone who's found. If the truth were known, a goodly number of us are wandering in spiritual circles and not making much headway. We're as spiritually detached this year as we were last year. We're looking into the New Year, and it doesn't really look like much is going to change.

For those of you who are still seekers, let me give you a word of encouragement. Chances are, God has already put a travel guide in your life somewhere. Chances are, if you were to scan the horizons of your relationships, you probably already know someone whose spiritual light burns pretty bright, whose love is real, whose faith has caught your attention more than once. That person may very well be God's gift to you—sort of like a Christmas star—God's travel guide.

Maybe you are saying, "Yeah, but it's just my wife, my kid, my neighbor, or my folks." You want to say, "Give me a laser-bright celestial travel guide, and *then* you'll have my full attention. But I don't want to take direction from a mere human being." To that, I say be careful and be humble. Let God determine the best way to lead you to His Son. The wise men would probably have preferred a more personalized kind of guidance, but the point is they were responsive to the guidance God provided. We should be, too, however it comes, through whomever it comes.

One day a businessman requested a meeting with me. He asked, "Bill, why doesn't life add up? Why don't the numbers really work out? Why does it all seem pointless? Why after fifty-five years do I feel more confused about the meaning of life instead of less confused?"

For the next half hour I was used by God in a way to be his travel guide. I said, "Life will add up only when you put Christ in the center of the equation. You use the map of His Word, and He'll lift the curtain of confusion and show you that all is not vanity or futility. He's in the transformation business, and He can transform your life."

You see, the key to this man's spiritual progress was that he sought out a travel guide and got a conversation going about spiritual matters.

Seekers, I challenge you to do the same kind of thing during the Christmas season. Identify the travel guide that God has already put in your life, and get a dialogue going with him or her. Ask your tough questions, express some of your deep doubts; initiate some interaction. But get on the road to finding Christ, and someday

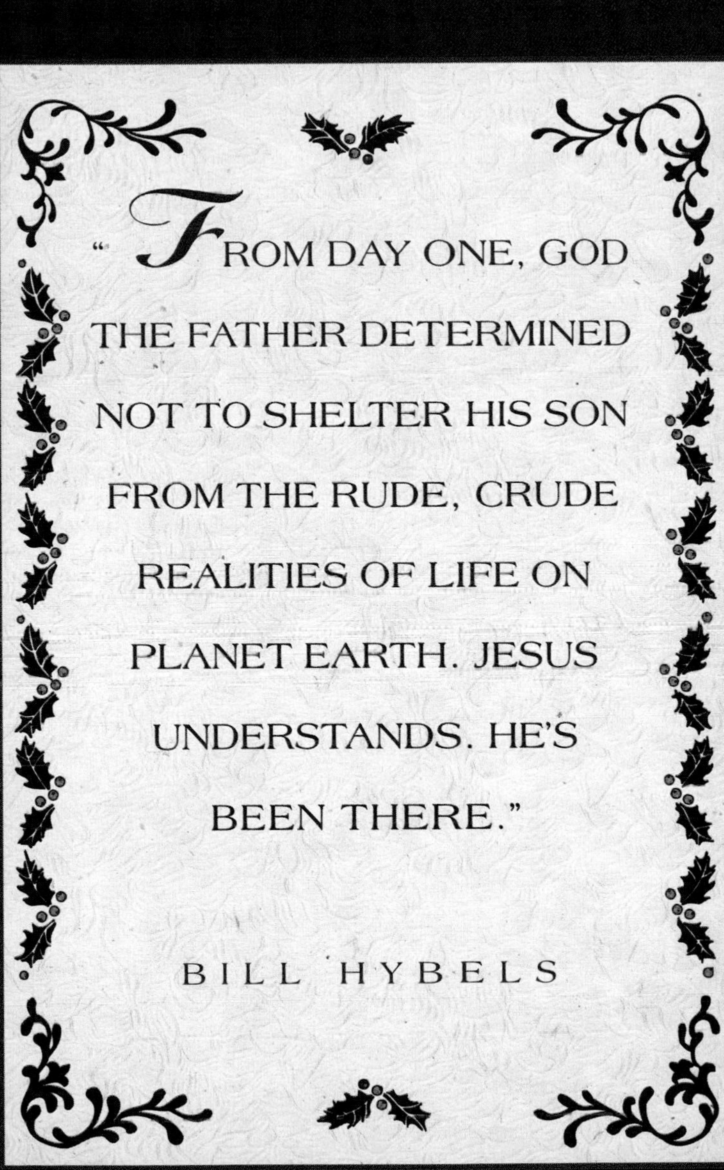
"FROM DAY ONE, GOD
THE FATHER DETERMINED
NOT TO SHELTER HIS SON
FROM THE RUDE, CRUDE
REALITIES OF LIFE ON
PLANET EARTH. JESUS
UNDERSTANDS. HE'S
BEEN THERE."
BILL HYBELS

you'll be awfully glad you did. Look at the star—God has probably given you one. Use it soon!

THE *STABLE*— GOD SENT JESUS TO LIVE IN THE *REAL WORLD*

Now refocus your zoom lens a little bit and look at the wooden stable itself, the rough-hewn hut that stablemakers always construct in a quaint, Christmasy style. Have you got the stable in focus? I can assure you the stable that Jesus was born in was anything but quaint. It was just like a thousand other stables, crowded with smelly animals, dark, damp, and rodent-infested. It was an all-around rotten place to birth a baby. Which makes a thinking person ask, "If God could commandeer a star to serve as a travel guide, why couldn't He commandeer a suite at the Bethlehem Hilton or at least a private room in the local hospital? The star is a much bigger feat than a suite would be." The answer is that God could have, but He made the deliberate choice not to.

God chose the stable for His Son to be born in for a very important reason. You see, when God sent His only Son to live on this earth, He made a strategic decision not to shelter Him from the harsh realities of this life. God had no intention of shielding His Son by having Him born into the make-believe world of the rich and famous.

God wanted His Son to experience life in its blue-collar boldness. Jesus' first breath of air burned with the odor of animal urine. The first noises He heard were the grunts of livestock. Jesus' first outfit was made of dust cloths, or the equivalent of grease rags. From day one, God the Father determined not to shelter His Son from the rude, crude realities of life on Planet Earth.

"Why?" you ask. "What was the purpose?" Let me ask you this: Can insulated aristocrats relate to what you and I go through? They don't live where we live, they don't eat like we eat, they don't work like we have to work, and they don't suffer like we suffer from time to time.

In Romania, an iron-fisted aristocrat lived in palatial splendor and told the common folk to eat cabbage. For twenty-four years the resentment grew inside the Romanians, until the people couldn't hold it in any longer. Not only did the common folk throw the dictator out of office—you saw it on your television sets—they broke into the palace and pitched his personal effects out into the street. People tore his material goods apart and spit on them. Then they stormed the palace and torched it.

You see, for twenty-four years the Romanians heard the guy's speeches and followed his orders and marched to his drumbeat, but underneath they kept muttering to themselves, "He's not one of us, he's not one of us." All along, as they did their menial tasks throughout the years, the Romanians had been saying, "You have no idea what we common folks are going through in this country. You have no idea. You live in a different world. You're sheltered and shielded."

Take a good look at the stable, friends. The stable is a permanent symbol of the fact that God sent Jesus to live in the real world.

For our sake, Jesus was given no aristocratic advantage. He had humbler beginnings than any of us. He was born into a real family, and He worked a real construction job for thirty years. He lived in a neighborhood. He had real friends. He suffered hardship like the rest of us have, and He died a cruel death for a crime He didn't commit.

So when the Bible urges people who are going through disappointment and pain to pour their hearts out to the now-ascended Savior, we Christians can do so with the absolute assurance that Jesus understands. He's been there.

Life without advantage? He lived it.

Shortage, poverty? He's been there.

Discrimination, oppression? Jesus was a refugee before His first birthday.

Rejection? He experienced it. Ridicule? It was a part of His daily life.

Abandonment? By lifelong friends in greatest time of need.

Death of loved ones? Multiple times.

Physical pain? More than you or I will probably ever experience.

Has some experience in your life driven you to within an inch of your breaking point? Has some experience hurt you so deeply that you've wanted to cry out, "I can't go on because nobody understands!"? If so, look at the stable. Be reminded this Christmas that Jesus understands. He's been there. He can identify with you no matter what you're going through. What's more, you matter to Him more than you can possibly imagine.

Can you see how important the stable is? It symbolizes the deliberately unsheltered life of Jesus. It stands as a monument to His ability to identify and sympathize with whatever we are going through. But we must be humble and trusting enough to pour out our hearts to Him and then allow Him to love and minister to us, and restore us to wholeness again. It almost becomes a cliché, but I'll say it again: The essence of Christianity is a relationship with a resurrected Savior. It's a dynamic restorative relationship, and it's with One who understands.

The *Manger*— The *Ordinary* Becomes *Extraordinary*

Well, you've seen the star, and you've seen the stable. Just refocus your zoom lens one last time and zero in on the manger. And please don't think of it as a first-century bassinet—it was a far cry from that. A manger was nothing more than a feed trough for cattle. It was just a crudely constructed piece of farm furniture—ordinary in every way.

If you think about it, the only reason twentieth-century Westerners are even familiar with the term *manger* is that a little clip of Scripture says God's Son was laid in one. Apart from that we wouldn't have a clue as to what a manger was. But because God's Son was laid in a manger, look what happened to an ordinary piece of farm furniture. All of a sudden it has a new dignity. It's a household word. The ordinary becomes extraordinary . . . a feed trough for cattle becomes the cradle of a king. That's quite a transformation. Wouldn't you agree?

Look at the manger. It is a symbol of what can happen to an ordinary man or woman when Jesus Christ resides inside. It's a symbol of what has happened to thousands of people around the world—ordinary people, average run-of-the-mill suburbanite people, here, there, and everywhere. Working, thinking, acting, relating people, until one day these ordinary people saw themselves for who they really were—lawbreakers in God's eyes. They saw themselves as sinners (and they were able to say the word *sinner*). They were moral failures, and they didn't hide from it. And they didn't tell themselves lies about it.

These ordinary people came to realize that they couldn't change their past record and they probably weren't going to change their future conduct. They knew that they would be standing guilty on judgment day. First, they fell on their knees in repentance. They were just ordinary people saying, "Oh, God, I see who I am. I see Your holiness, and I know I've fallen short. I repent, Lord; on my knees, I repent!"

Second, they fell on their knees to cry out for grace. They pleaded for the grace that only God can give through His Son, the Christmas child, who was born to die for the sins of the world.

Third, they fell to their knees in worship to Christ when they realized that salvation had been granted and forgiveness had been afforded them. Their record had been dealt with, and reconciliation with God had become a reality. They were now adopted, forgiven, and brought into the family of God as sons and daughters. That's cause for a time of worship on bended knee.

Ordinary people fell on their knees and cried out, "Oh, God, thank You for Jesus Christ. Thank You for who He was and what He did for me." When Jesus Christ takes up residency, by His Spirit, in an ordinary life, I can assure you the ordinary gives way to the extraordinary. Just as a feed trough becomes a king's cradle, a very average man or woman becomes exceptional through responsiveness to God.

Where he was once only a people-pleaser, a man now becomes concerned about giving God pleasure. Where she was once self-absorbed, a woman now becomes exceptional in love for other people, in thoughtfulness, generosity, tenderness, and purity. You see, God does to humans what Jesus did to the manger. He makes something that was ordinary extraordinary.

What about you? Will you allow Jesus to bring about that kind of transformation in your life, if He hasn't already?

Wherever you go at Christmastime, you're going to see nativity scenes. When you pass one in your car, look at the star. God provides travel guides for earnest seekers.

Look at the stable. Don't ever forget that God decided not to shelter His Son. He let Him go through all of what you and I experience so

He could be a sympathetic Savior. He understands.

Look at the manger, an ordinary piece of farm furniture transformed into a King's cradle.

You know, your choice is simple. You can just stand there and watch another nativity scene go by. Or you can fall on your knees in repentance, and then in worship.

What will you choose to do this Christmas?

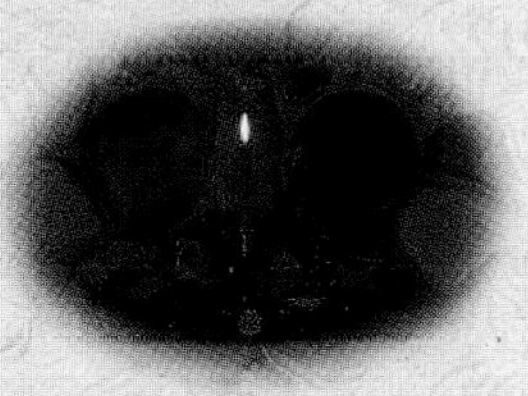

"When they saw the star,

they rejoiced with

exceedingly great joy."

MATTHEW 2:10 NKJV

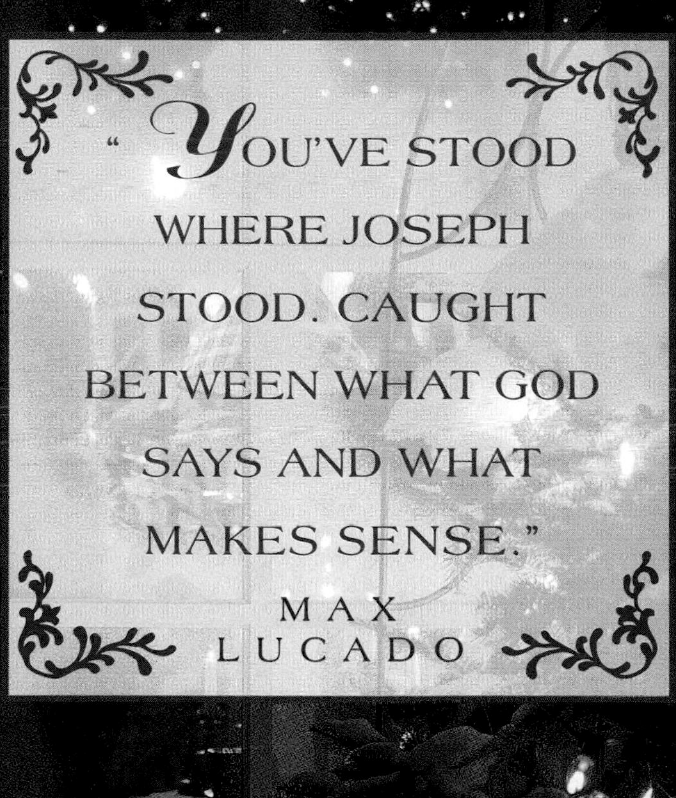
"YOU'VE STOOD
WHERE JOSEPH
STOOD. CAUGHT
BETWEEN WHAT GOD
SAYS AND WHAT
MAKES SENSE."
MAX
LUCADO

MAX LUCADO

Joseph's PRAYER

oseph . . . did what the Lord's angel had told him to do. (Matthew 1:24 NCV)

The white space between Bible verses is fertile soil for questions. One can hardly read Scripture without whispering, "I wonder . . . "

"I wonder if Eve ever ate any more fruit."

"I wonder if Noah slept well during storms."

"I wonder if Jonah liked fish or if Jeremiah had friends."

"Did Moses avoid bushes? Did Jesus tell jokes? Did Peter ever try water-walking again?"

"Would any woman have married Paul had he asked?"

The Bible is a fence full of knotholes through which we can peek but not see the whole picture. It's a scrapbook of snapshots capturing people in encounters with God, but not always recording the result. So we wonder:

When the woman caught in adultery went home, what did she say to her husband?

After the demoniac was delivered, what did he do for a living?

After Jairus's daughter was raised from the dead, did she ever regret it?

Knotholes and snapshots and "I wonders." You'll find them in every chapter about every person. But nothing stirs so many questions as does the birth of Christ. Characters appear and disappear before we can ask them anything. The innkeeper too busy to welcome God—did he ever learn who he turned away? The shepherds—did they ever hum the song the angels sang? The wise men who followed the star—what was it like to worship a toddler? And Joseph, especially Joseph. I've got questions for Joseph.

Did you and Jesus arm wrestle? Did he ever let you win?

Did you ever look up from your prayers and see Jesus listening?

How do you say "Jesus" in Egyptian?

What ever happened to the wise men?

What ever happened to you?

We don't know what happened to Joseph.

His role in Act I is so crucial that we expect to see him the rest of the drama—but with the exception of a short scene with twelve-year-old Jesus in Jerusalem, he never reappears. The rest of his life is left to speculation, and we are left with our questions.

But of all my questions, my first would be about Bethlehem. I'd like to know about the night in the stable. I can picture Joseph there. Moonlit pastures. Stars twinkle above. Bethlehem sparkles in the distance. There he is, pacing outside the stable.

What was he thinking while Jesus was being born? What was on his mind while Mary was giving birth? He'd done all he could do—heated the water, prepared a place for Mary to lie. He'd made Mary as comfortable as she could be in a barn and then he stepped out. She'd asked to be alone, and Joseph has never felt more so.

In that eternity between his wife's dismissal and Jesus' arrival, what was he thinking? He walked into the night and looked into the stars. Did he pray?

For some reason, I don't see him silent; I see Joseph animated, pacing. Head shaking one minute, fist shaking the next. This isn't what he had in mind. I wonder what he said . . .

This isn't the way I *planned* it, God. Not at all. My child being born in a stable? This isn't the way I thought it would be. A cave with sheep and donkeys, hay and straw? My wife giving birth with only the stars to hear her pain?

This isn't at all what I imagined. No, I imagined family. I imagined grandmothers. I imagined neighbors clustered outside the door and friends standing at my side. I imagined the house erupting with the first cry of the infant. Slaps on the back. Loud laughter. Jubilation.

That's how I thought it would be.

The midwife would hand me my child and all the people would applaud. Mary would rest and we would celebrate. All of Nazareth would celebrate.

But now. Now look. Nazareth is five days' journey away. And here we are in a . . . in a sheep pasture. Who will celebrate with us? The sheep? The shepherds? The stars?

This doesn't seem right. What kind of husband am I? I provide no midwife to aid my wife. No bed to rest her back. Her pillow is a blanket from my donkey. My house for her is a shed of hay and straw.

The smell is bad, the animals are loud. Why, I even smell like a shepherd myself.

Did I *miss* something? Did I, God?

When you sent the angel and spoke of the son being born—this isn't what I pictured. I envisioned Jerusalem, the temple, the priests, and the people gathered to watch. A pageant perhaps. A parade. A banquet at least. I mean, this is the Messiah!

Or, if not born in Jerusalem, how about Nazareth? Wouldn't Nazareth have been better? At least there I have my house and my business. Out here, what do I have? A weary mule, a stack of firewood, and a pot of warm water. This is not the way I wanted it to be! This is not the way I wanted my son.

Oh my, I did it again. I did it again, didn't I, Father? I don't mean to do that; it's just that I forget. He's not my son . . . he's yours.

The child is yours. The plan is yours. The idea is yours. And forgive me for asking but . . . Is this how God enters the world? The coming of the angel, I've accepted. The questions people asked about the pregnancy, I can tolerate. The trip to Bethlehem, fine. But why a birth in a stable, God?

Any minute now Mary will give birth. Not to a child, but to the Messiah. Not to an infant, but to God. That's what the angel said. That's what Mary believes. And, God, my God, that's what I want to believe. But surely you can understand; it's not easy. It seems so . . . so . . . so . . . bizarre.

I'm unaccustomed to such strangeness, God. I'm a carpenter. I make things fit. I square off the edges. I follow the plumb line. I measure

"GOD STILL LOOKS FOR JOSEPHS TODAY. MEN AND WOMEN WHO BELIEVE THAT GOD IS NOT THROUGH WITH THIS WORLD. COMMON PEOPLE WHO SERVE AN UNCOMMON GOD."

MAX LUCADO

twice before I cut once. Surprises are not the friend of a builder. I like to know the plan. I like to see the plan before I begin.

But this time I'm not the builder, am I? This time I'm a tool. A hammer in your grip. A nail between your fingers. A chisel in your hands. This project is yours, not mine.

I guess it's foolish of me to question you. Forgive my struggling. Trust doesn't come easy to me, God. But you never said it would be easy, did you?

One final thing, Father. The angel you sent? Any chance you could send another? If not an angel, maybe a person? I don't know anyone around here and some company would be nice. Maybe the innkeeper or a traveler? Even a shepherd would do.

I wonder. Did Joseph ever pray such a prayer? Perhaps he did. Perhaps he didn't.

But you probably have.

You've stood where Joseph stood. Caught between what God says and what makes sense.

You've done what he told you to do only to wonder if it was him speaking in the first place. You've stared into a sky blackened with doubt. And you've asked what Joseph asked.

You've asked if you're still on the right road. You've asked if you were supposed to turn left when you turned right. And you've asked if there is a plan behind this scheme. Things haven't turned out like you thought they would.

Each of us knows what it's like to search the night for light. Not outside a stable, but perhaps outside an emergency room. On the gravel of a roadside. On the manicured grass of a cemetery. We've asked our questions. We questioned God's plan. And we've wondered why God does what he does.

The Bethlehem sky is not the first to hear the pleading of a confused pilgrim.

If you are asking what Joseph asked, let me urge you to do what Joseph did. Obey. That's what he did. He obeyed. He obeyed when the angel called. He obeyed when Mary explained. He obeyed when God sent.

He was obedient to God.

He was obedient when the sky was bright.

He was obedient when the sky was dark.

He didn't let his confusion disrupt his obedience. He didn't know everything. But he did what he knew. He shut down his business, packed up his family, and went to another country. Why? Because that's what God said to do.

What about You? Just like Joseph, you can't see the whole picture. Just like Joseph your task is to see that Jesus is brought into your part of your world. And just like Joseph you have a choice: to obey or disobey. Because Joseph obeyed, God used him to change the world.

Can he do the same with you?

God still looks for Josephs today. Men and women who believe that God is not through with this world. Common people who serve an uncommon God.

Will you be that kind of person? Will you serve . . . even when you don't understand?

No, the Bethlehem sky is not the first to hear the pleadings of an honest heart, nor the last. And perhaps God didn't answer every question for Joseph. But he answered the most important one. "Are you still with me, God?" And through the first cries of the God-child the answer came.

"Yes. Yes, Joseph. I'm with you."

There are many questions about the Bible that we won't be able to answer until we get home. Many knotholes and snapshots. Many times we will muse, "I wonder . . ."

But in our wonderings, there is one question we never need to ask. Does God care? Do we matter to God? Does he still love his children?

Through the small face of the stable-born baby, he says yes.

Yes, your sins are forgiven.

Yes, your name is written in heaven.

Yes, death has been defeated.

And yes, God has entered your world.

Immanuel. God is with us.

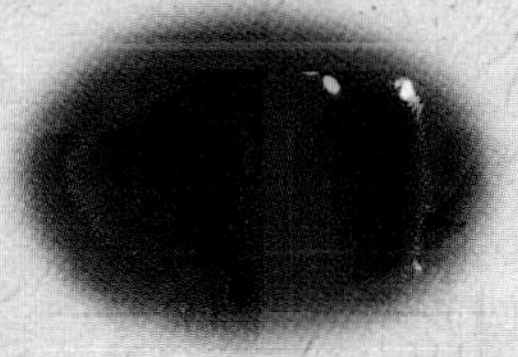

"Joseph . . . did what the Lord's angel had told him to do."

MATTHEW 1:24 NCV

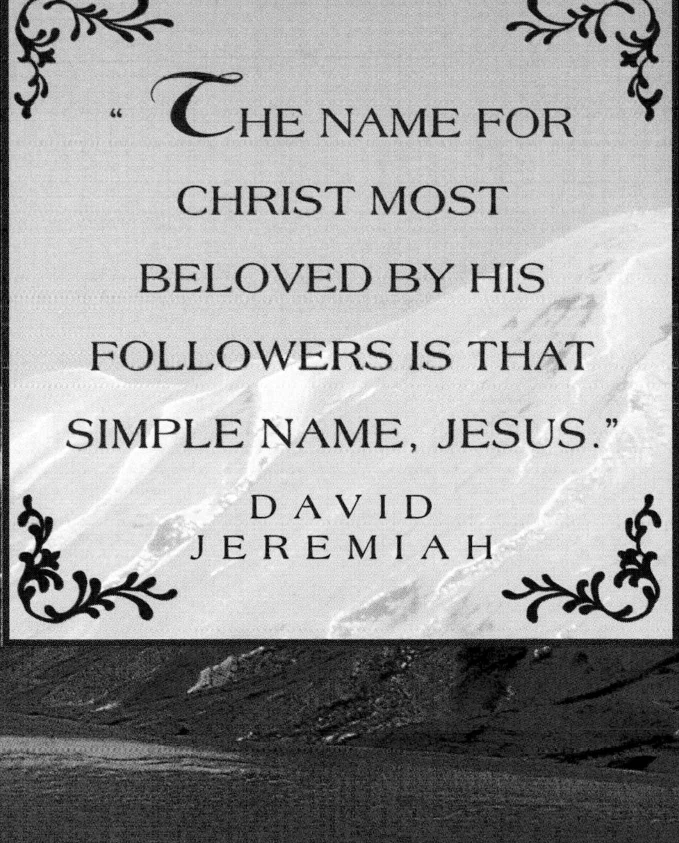
"THE NAME FOR
CHRIST MOST
BELOVED BY HIS
FOLLOWERS IS THAT
SIMPLE NAME, JESUS."
DAVID
JEREMIAH

DAVID JEREMIAH

Thou Shalt CALL HIS NAME JESUS

've been blessed with a very interesting name. My dear friend Tory Johnson used to be the head of a Bible conference that I visited every year. I shall never forget the first time I met Tory. He got up to introduce me, and he said, "We are very fortunate today to have with us a man who represents much of the Old Testament. He is a prophet by the name of Jeremiah, and he is also a shepherd and king by the name of David. But it is truly too bad that in this New Testament age, he doesn't have any link with the New Testament Scriptures."

I had the joy of standing up and telling him that my full name is David *Paul* Jeremiah. From that day until this, whenever I see Tory Johnson he calls me David Paul Jeremiah. The only other person who ever did that was my mother—when I was in trouble.

The names we give to our children often take a great deal of thought on our part, and they sometimes even cause a few arguments along the way. It's interesting how we come up with names, isn't it? Even in today's culture, the name sometimes comes from the father's name. In the New Testament Scriptures, names were often based upon who the father was—a child was called someone's son. We still see that in our modern world, although we probably don't even think of it. For instance, we know about Thompson and Johnson and Peterson and Jackson, and many others. Those are names that got into the English language because somebody was the son of Tom, or the son of Peter, or the son of Jack, so that name became his name.

Sometimes a name is chosen because the child has a special meaning in the family. That is often the case in the Scriptures. In the Bible, people chose names with care. The Hebrews placed far more meaning on the names they gave their children than we do today. So when it was time for God to clothe His Son in humanity, how He would name Him became very important. What name would He give to His Son, who was to be born of a virgin, into the home of Joseph and Mary? What woul Him?

It's interesting that God did not leave naming of His Son up to the earthly paren Instead, He sent an angel to make sure Joseph got it right. In Matthew 1:21, the angel is speaking to Joseph, comforting his fear, because Joseph does not understand what is going on with Mary at all: "And she will bring forth a Son, and you shall call His name Jesus, for He will save His people from their sins" (Matt. 1:21 NKJV).

By special instruction, expressing God's perfect will, it came to pass in Bethlehem. While the stars were shining, and the angels were singing, and the wise men were somewhere journeying, someone asked, "Who is that in the manger?"

Mary and Joseph responded, "His name is Jesus."

Did you know that in the Gospels, God's Son is called by that particular name over 500 times? In fact, the word *Jesus* appears throughout the New Testament 909 times. You get the impression it's the favorite and most endearing term for our Lord. Of all the names and of all the titles that are given to Christ, the one most beloved by His followers is that simple name, Jesus.

If you glance through a hymnal, you will discover that the writers have memorialized that name in hymns we love to sing. John Newton gave us "How Sweet the Name of Jesus Sounds." We also have the wonderful hymn "All Hail the Power of Jesus' Name." Bernard leads us to devotional depths with "Jesus, the Very Thought of Thee." Baxter admonishes us, "Take the Name of Jesus with You." And we sometimes sing, "Oh, How I Love Jesus." There are so many hymns about Jesus that I could never name them all.

If ever a name was designed to indicate the most significant thing about the person to whom it was given, then God in heaven knew what He was doing when He named His Son Jesus. *Jesus* means "Jehovah Saves" or "The Lord of Salvation." And that is who He is—the Salvation of the

Lord. I would like to suggest to you some reasons why the name Jesus is so important and perfect. And I'd like to share with you, as we enter into this Christmas season, why Jesus is my favorite of all the names for our Lord.

Jesus Is an *Easy* Name

Do you know there was a man in the Bible named Tiglath Pelezer-Adonibezek? Aren't you glad God didn't call His Son that? I mean, can you imagine the worship choruses we might have written around that name? Instead, God called His Son Jesus. Only two syllables, five letters, pronounced the same in almost any language. A child can learn it. It was a common Hebrew name, a popular one in Jewish families at the time our Lord was born. "Jesus" in the New Testament is the same as "Joshua" in the Old Testament.

If you translate this name into all the languages and dialects of the world, whether Hebrew, Greek, or Anglo-Saxon, you cannot rob it of its music. Its sweet tones break in upon your ear. I often enjoy listening to shortwave radio, and I have found many missionary stations around the globe. Sometimes I'll hear a tune I recognize, but I can't understand the words because they're in a different language. But if I listen long enough, I'll hear Jesus' name. And even though I don't know the language, I can say, "Well, I know *that* word." In any language, the name Jesus has a sameness about it, even though the inflections and the structure are different. You can pick Jesus' name out of almost every language. It is a universal symbol of the love of God for His people. It is a simple name. Some poet has written,

Jesus, the name high over all.
In hell, on earth and sky.
Angels and man before it fall;
And devils fear and fly.

Jesus, oh the magic
Of the soft love sound.
How it thrills and trembles
To creation's bound.
Unknown

God said to the angel, "When you go down there to see Joseph, you make sure to tell him the baby's name is Jesus." The name was registered in heaven so that it belonged, specifically, to the Son of God.

As I mentioned before, Bernard of Clairvaux wrote the words to "Jesus, the Very Thought of Thee." Have you ever thought about those words? They were written many years ago, and the language may sound a little bit stilted. Yet they convey so beautifully the thought of the precious name of Jesus:

Nor voice can sing, Nor heart can frame,
Nor can the mem'ry find
A sweeter sound than Thy blest name,
O Savior of mankind!

Another hymn writer penned,

Jesus, O how sweet the Name.
Jesus, every day the same.
Jesus, let all saints proclaim,
His worthy praise forever.

If they grow up in a Christian environment, our children learn the name Jesus almost as soon as they learn to say Mamma and Daddy. And have you ever noticed that children think Jesus is the answer to every question? I remember the story about a little boy who was asked in class to describe a little furry animal that climbs up in a tree and eats nuts and saves acorns. This little boy, who was brought up in a Christian home, said, "It sounds like a squirrel, but I know the right answer is Jesus." God has given to us a Savior whose name is so simple and easy that a child can learn to say it: "His name shall be called Jesus."

"GOD KNEW WHAT HE WAS DOING WHEN HE NAMED HIS SON. *JESUS* MEANS 'JEHOVAH SAVES' OR 'THE LORD OF SALVATION.' AND THAT IS WHO HE IS—THE SALVATION OF THE LORD."

DAVID JEREMIAH

Jesus Is an *Esteemed* Name

According to Josephus, there are eleven men in the Old Testament with the name Joshua, the Hebrew translation of Jesus. And no parents had ever called their children by that name until Moses created a name for a man who was formerly called Hoshea: "These are the names of the men whom Moses sent to spy out the land. And Moses called Hoshea the son of Nun, Joshua" (Num. 13:16 NKJV).

Now *Hoshea* means "salvation." And *Jehovah* means "Lord." So when Moses changed Hoshea's name to "Joshua," he gave him a name of redemption, a name that sounds like some sort of a savior. And he was, wasn't he?

Many Bible scholars consider Joshua of the Old Testament to be a picture of Christ. And, if you think about it, there are some striking points of comparison between the two. Joshua led the Israelites out of the wilderness to the promised land. Jesus, as our Savior, brings us from the wilderness of sin into the spiritual promised land. In the Old Testament, Joshua led his people to conquer enemies who were protected by walled cities and huge giants. Jesus leads us to conquer the enemies of our soul. He enables us to fight victoriously against all of life's most difficult obstacles and its giants of temptation, trial, and testing. As our Joshua, Jesus leads us to the inheritance that God has for us.

Joshua's salvation was earthly and temporal, but the salvation that Jesus came to bring is heavenly and eternal, and it never needs to be purchased for us again. In fact, the writer of the book of Hebrews puts these two men together in a wonderful little statement in Hebrews 4:8 (NKJV): "For if Joshua had given them rest, then He would not afterward have spoken of another day."

In other words, if Joshua could have done the salvation work for the people, there would have been no need for another Joshua in terms of Jesus. But Joshua could only work in the material world; so there remained a need for the New Testament Jesus to be born, so that we could be saved from our sin.

Jesus Is an *Enduring* Name

Did you know that even though our Lord Jesus was born in obscurity over two thousand years ago and died like a criminal at the age of thirty-three, His name is the most well-known name in history? We pass it on from age to age, in printed page and spoken word. It is the most wonderful name in all the world.

At Christmas we all observe a kind of irony: The people who most angrily protest Jesus Christ and what He stands for, and who most blatantly oppose all that Christ has come to do through His people and Church, nevertheless march along in celebration of His birthday. Have you ever gone to a birthday celebration for somebody you just don't like at all? We're not supposed to have enemies, but let's suppose you have an archenemy, and you were invited to his birthday party. Would you go? Absolutely not! You would not go. You would wonder why you got an invitation. But the enemies of the Lord go to His birthday party every year, don't they? Isn't that something? The writer of the book of Revelation tells us: "They shall see His face, and His name shall be on their foreheads" (22:4 NKJV).

Jesus Is an *Exalted* Name

In two passages in Paul's letters, he speaks of the name of Jesus. In Ephesians we read, "He raised Him from the dead and seated Him at His right hand in the heavenly places, far above all principality and power and might and dominion, and every name that is named, not only in this age but also in that which is to come" (1:20–21 NKJV).

Turn over just a few pages in your New Testament to the book of Philippians, the second chapter. This is one of the great New Testament passages, and it is often taught at the Christmas season: "Therefore God also has highly exalted Him and given Him the name which is above every name, that at the name of Jesus every knee should bow, of those in heaven, and of those on earth, and of those under the earth, and that every tongue should confess that Jesus Christ is Lord, to the glory of God the Father" (Phil. 2:9–11 NKJV).

Jesus Is an *Exclusive* Name

When the angel said to Joseph, "You shall call His name Jesus," he added a qualifying phrase to set the name apart: "You shall call His name Jesus, for *He will save His people from their sins*." The Joshua of the Old Testament couldn't do that. Would-be saviors around Christendom have claimed the ability to do it, but there is no one who can forgive sin but Jesus alone. A priest can't forgive sin. As a pastor, I cannot forgive sin. There is no man on earth who can forgive sin, but Jesus can. He came to save His people from their sin. Because of that, He is the most unique Person in the universe. His name is above every name, and His purpose in coming to this earth sets Him apart from everyone, for He saves His people from their sins. Do you believe that? "Nor is there salvation in any other, for there is no other name under heaven given among men by which we must be saved" (Acts 4:12 NKJV).

If someone comes to you and says salvation is here or over there, don't you believe it. The Bible says there is only one way to God, and that's through Jesus Christ. Oh, how much abuse we take for teaching that scriptural principle! All the religions of the world feel that Christians are narrow and exclusive. I don't like to be called narrow-minded any more than you do, but I do want to be just as narrow-minded as the Bible is. I want to be just as straightforward and exclusive as is the Scripture. The Word of God says, "Narrow is the way, which leads unto God. Broad is the way that leads to destruction." Having a broad mind could get you in the wrong place, my friend.

Jesus is the only way. When God sent His angel to Joseph and said, "Call Him Jesus because He's going to save His people from their sins," He set Jesus apart from all other humans. He is the only One who can save.

Salvation is not in the Baptist Church. It's not in the Methodist Church. It's not in the Catholic Church or the Charismatic Church. Salvation is found in the name of the Lord Jesus Christ. And if you're not trusting in the name of the Lord Jesus Christ, your trust is misplaced. You are going to end up in a place where you do not want to go. His name is exclusive. A poet has written it this way:

There is majesty in the name God.
There is personality in the name Jehovah.
There is power in the name Lord.
There is unction in the name Christ.
There is affinity in the name Immanuel.
There is intercession in the name Mediator.
There is help in the name Advocate.
But there is salvation in none other,
None under heaven given among men,
Apart from the name Jesus.
An Alexander may build an empire.
A Napoleon may change the nations of the world.
A Newton may bring about an intellectual revolution.
An Edison may create a new world for science.
A Wyatt may usher in a new era of industry.
But there is only one who can touch and transform the human heart.
And that one is Jesus.

Unknown

Jesus is the only One who can save us from our sins. When I preach about Jesus in a church or some other gathering and people hear and open their hearts, their lives are changed. Can you think of anything more amazing and miraculous than that? When I preach about Jesus on the radio and people hear it in their car, Jesus comes into their hearts and changes their lives.

Two truckers came up to talk to me in Montana some time ago—one on one night and one on another. They each told me that they were driving down the highway when they turned on their radio and heard about Jesus. They pulled their trucks off the highway and bowed their heads in their cabs, and received Jesus Christ into their life. And they told me, "He's changed my life." Jesus does that.

Perhaps you've tried everything else in the world. You've tried self-improvement courses, education, and support groups of all different kinds. You might be a little more sophisticated, but you're in the same mess you were in before you started. Why? Because there's only One who can change your life, and His name is Jesus.

You know why His change works? He doesn't change us from the outside in; He changes us from the inside out. Somebody told me that the problem with a lot of people today is that they don't have the reality on the inside, so they have to make a big deal about everything on the outside. Have you ever known people like that? They parade their religion. They walk around acting like they're something they're not, because they don't have the real thing in their hearts. But Jesus comes to your heart to change you from the inside out. If you've never been touched by the power of Jesus, then you don't know what it means to truly know God. If you know Jesus, He can change your life.

I know a soul that is steeped in sin,
That no man's art can cure.
But I know a name, a name, a name,
That can make the soul all pure.

I know a life that's lost to God,
Bound down by the things of the earth,
But I know a name, a name, a name,
That can bring that soul new birth.

Unknown

What is the name of the Christmas baby? The name of God's only begotten Son? The name of the One who can save us from our sins? His name is Jesus.

Jesus. Oh, how sweet the name!

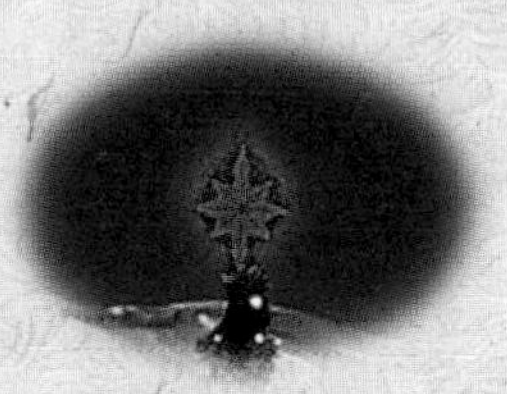

"You shall call His name

Jesus, for He will save

His people from their sins."

MATTHEW 1:21 NKJV

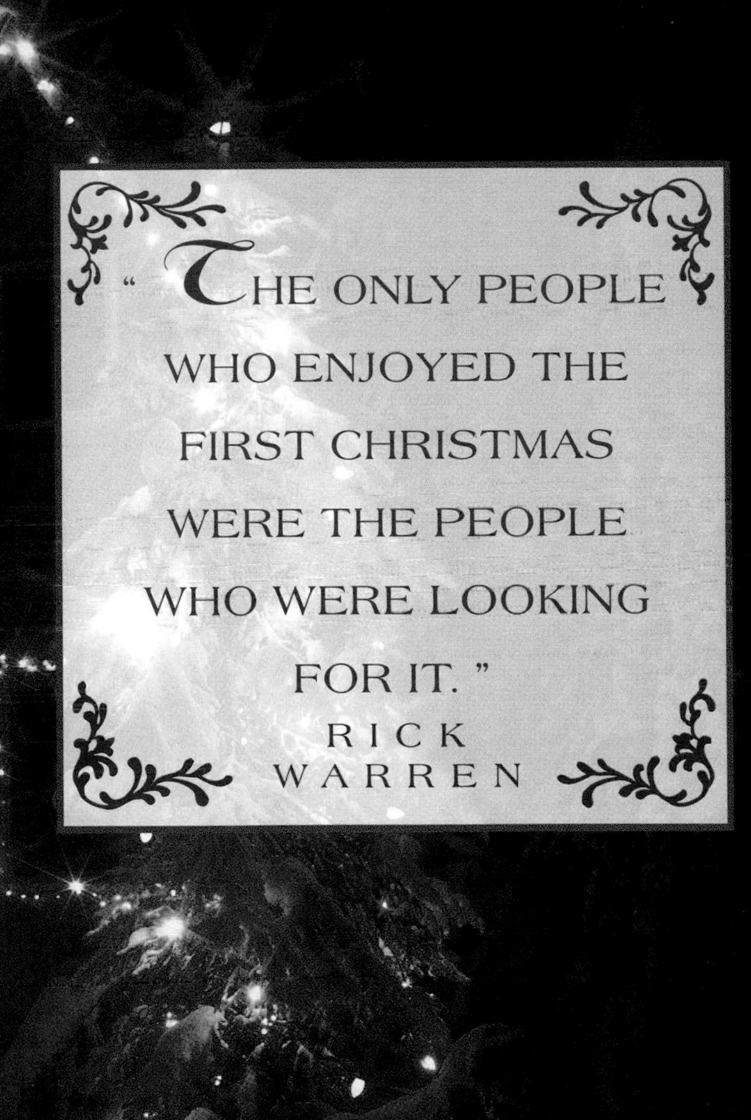
"THE ONLY PEOPLE
WHO ENJOYED THE
FIRST CHRISTMAS
WERE THE PEOPLE
WHO WERE LOOKING
FOR IT."
RICK
WARREN

RICK WARREN

What Will You FIND AT CHRISTMAS?

hat do you want for Christmas this year? If you were to ask a typical little boy, he'd give you two words: *Power Rangers*. There's a little boy I know named Brian. For weeks he bugged his parents about getting a watch for Christmas. Finally his dad told him, "Brian, if you mention that watch again, you're not going to get it. Quit bugging us!"

One night Brian's parents asked him to lead in prayer before dinner.

Brian said, "I'd like to quote a Scripture verse before I pray. Mark 13:37: 'I say unto you what I have already told you before—watch . . .'"

Now that is appropriate use of Scripture!

You know, we spend most of our Christmas season searching for the perfect gift, the huge bargain, the ideal decoration, the last parking spot. At the very first Christmas, many people missed it because they were too busy looking for other things. The politicians missed the first Christmas. The business community missed the first Christmas. The innkeeper missed the first

Christmas. Even the religious establishment missed the first Christmas, because they were looking at other things. The only people who enjoyed the very first Christmas, nearly two thousand years ago, were the people who were looking for it.

> Angels: "You'll find the baby . . . lying in a manger."
> Shepherds: "Let's go and see!" (See Luke 2:12, 15)

The shepherds found Jesus because they were searching. They were seeking Him. And later on, another group, the wise men, found Jesus because they were looking for Him, too.

> Wise men came from the East, asking, "Where is the baby . . . ? We have come to worship Him." (See Matt. 2:1–2)

Now let me ask you: What are you going to find this Christmas? I'll tell you what you're going to find: *You'll find what you're looking for.*

Seek, and you will find. (Matt. 7:7 NKJV)

I don't know if you've caught it or not, but in our society today there's a new emphasis on seeking spiritual truth. The media have caught it. Look through some fairly recent issues of *Time, Life, Newsweek,* and *U.S. News and World Report* and you'll see what I mean. One has a "Life After Death" cover story. Another offers a "Clear View of Heaven." *Life* magazine asks, "Who Was He?" with a picture of Jesus on the cover. *U.S. News* covers the question "Who Wrote the Bible?" One magazine boldly implies that it can answer the question "Who Is God?" Meanwhile, "The Search for the Sacred," is detailed in *Newsweek.*

Clearly, publishers don't put these kinds of covers on their publications unless they sell magazines. Which means there is an intense interest in spiritual things in our society.

The *Newsweek* article "The Search for the Sacred" says this: "Maybe it's just a critical mass of Baby Boomers in the contemplative afternoon of life. Or maybe it's anxiety over the coming millennium, or maybe it's a general dissatisfaction with the materialism of the modern world. For these reasons and more, millions of Americans are embarking on a search for the sacred in their lives."

The bottom line is that people are asking, "Is there any meaning to my life? Does my life count? Is there a God? And if there is a God, can I get to know Him?" That's what Christmas is all about—getting to know God.

In response, God says, "I know everything about you: the good, the bad, the ugly, your past, present, future." He wants you to know Him, so He sent Jesus at Christmas.

Later on the article reports, "A lot has changed in the past century. We've stripped away what once our ancestors saw as essential, the importance of religion in the family, and people feel they want something they've lost; they just don't remember what it is they've lost."

In essence, people have a gaping hole in their souls, and that is a seeker's quest—to fill the hole with a new source of meaning. Why are we here? What is the purpose of our existence? Now, if you're honest with yourself, at least during some time of your life, when you've slowed down long enough, you've probably asked yourself those same questions. At least they've popped into your mind. "Why am I here? What am I here for? Why do I exist? Why should I get up in the morning, go to work, come home, watch TV, and go to bed? Is there any purpose in that? Is there a God? Can God be known?"

Where do you think those ideas are coming from? God is putting those questions in your mind because He's creating a desire in you—a thirst to know Him. God knows all about you; He wants you to know Him. And there's no better time than Christmas to become the kind of seeker the wise men embodied. Wise people still seek Christ.

This Christmas God wants to give you three Christmas gifts that you'll find if you seek them. Because whatever you're looking for is what you'll find.

This Christmas, You Can Find *Forgiveness*

Today your Savior was born . . . He is Christ, the Lord. (Luke 2:11 NCV)

Circle that word *Savior*. That's what Christmas is all about. But why do we need a Savior anyway? Well, let me just cut to the chase. The Bible says that heaven is a perfect place. There are no mistakes or inconsistencies; it is perfect. Because of that, only perfect people get to go there. If God let imperfect people into heaven, it wouldn't be perfect anymore. That means I don't stand a chance in a million of getting into heaven on my own effort, and neither do you. I lost my chance at perfection a long time ago. So God had to come up with "Plan B." He sent us a Savior so we could get in on somebody else's ticket. That's the good news: A Savior has been born!

A little boy wrote a letter to Santa Claus that said, "Dear Santa: There are three boys living at my house. Jeffrey is two, David is four, and Norman is seven. Jeffrey is good some of the time, David is good some of the time, and Norman is good *all* of the time. I am Norman."

You know the problem with that? Not one of us is a Norman. None of us bat 1000. None of us are always perfect or right. In fact, if we had a giant screen up behind us and were able to view everything we've ever thought, said, or done, most of us would be extremely embarrassed. We all live with a sense of regret because none of us are perfect. That's why we need a Savior.

Not long ago, I saw a little Christmas card

that said, "If our greatest need had been information, God would have sent an educator. If our greatest need had been technology, God would have sent a scientist. If our greatest need had been money, God would have sent an economist. If our greatest need had been pleasure, God would have sent us an entertainer. But our greatest need was forgiveness, so He sent us a Savior."

"Unto you is born a Savior." Yes, you can be forgiven. Now that's the most priceless gift you can get, the gift of a clear conscience. You can't even buy that at Nieman-Marcus; it's priceless. Yet at Christmastime God offers you the chance to have your past forgiven and wiped clean, so you can start over, brand new. That's good news!

Now, how do I let Christ save me? It's really simple. Relax and look at this: "All who believe in Jesus will be forgiven of their sins through Jesus' name" (Acts 10:43 NCV).

Notice that it simply says "*all* who believe." *All* means you. You just let go. Do you know how you get Christ to save you? Just admit you need Him to do so.

For three years I was a lifeguard. They fired me because every time I saw somebody raise their hand because they were drowning I said, "Yes, I see that hand! God bless you! Is there another? Yes, God bless you, too!"

Okay, I made up that part, but I really was a lifeguard. And one of the things that all lifeguards know is that you can't save anybody as long as they're trying to save themselves, because they'll take you under the water with them. You swim out to them, and they're flailing around in the water until finally they just give up and collapse. Once they give up, it's really easy—you just put your arm over their shoulder and swim back to shore. There's nothing to it. But you can't save them as long as they're trying to save themselves.

You know our problem? We're always trying to save ourselves. We think we can work our way into heaven. We say, "Oh, God, my good works are so high, and my bad works are so low. Look at the difference!" The only problem is that God doesn't grade on a curve. He says, "Only perfect people need apply for a perfect place." You might say, "Well, I'm better than Hitler." Well of course you are—you're better than me, too. I have no doubt about that. But God doesn't judge you against anybody else. So you need a Savior. And that is provided. It's a free gift; just accept it.

This Christmas You Can Find *Peace of Mind*

Those who love your teachings will find true peace. (Ps. 119:165 NCV)

Peace is a word that our world uses a lot, but most people don't have the foggiest idea of its true meaning. That's worth repeating: Our society hasn't got the slightest idea what genuine peace of mind is all about.

For many, peace of mind means drinking

until they're so drunk and numb that they can no longer feel the pain in their hearts.

For some, peace means hopping from one relationship to the next, to the next, to the next, hoping that somebody will fill the void in their life. But nobody ever does.

For some, peace means staying busy all the time so that at night they just kind of collapse into bed and don't have to think. Because any time they're quiet, those haunting thoughts, those fears, and that terrible loneliness come caving in, and they don't like that feeling.

For other people peace means working and working, becoming a workaholic and overachieving, so they can get all these attributes of success to prove to the world that they're somebody! But inside they're saying, "I don't really feel like somebody."

For other people peace means trying New Age gimmicks, like gazing at crystals, or using aromatherapy, or sitting in a lotus position and contemplating lint in their navel and going, "Ommmmm." But that's not peace of mind, either.

Let me tell you what real peace of mind is. Real peace of mind is having a relationship with Jesus Christ, God's Son, and becoming friends with God.

Real peace is knowing that no matter what I do, God will never stop loving me.

Real peace is knowing that no matter what happens, God will never leave me alone. He'll always be with me.

Real peace means that no matter what happens in the New Year, or in the years to come, I know that God is going to give me the strength to handle it.

Real peace is living by God's Word, the Bible, so I can avoid a lot of the needless hang-ups and hurts and habits that mess up my life.

Real peace is teaching my children God's Word as a foundation for life, so as I see them make decisions, I can say, "Boy, I'm proud of that! I wasn't even there, and my kids made that decision on their own." That's real peace.

There are three things that rob us of peace of mind: *guilt*, *grief*, and *grudges*. First there's guilt. You don't have to walk around with guilt. God said, "I sent a Savior to wipe away your sins so you can be forgiven." Jesus gives us a clear conscience, like an Etch-A-Sketch. If you haven't been cleansed from your sins by placing your faith in Jesus, guilt will rob you of your peace.

Grief also robs us. You may be in major pain right now, because Christmastime brings up all kinds of hurtful memories. You may remember the loss of a loved one, or a parent who abandoned you, or a divorce you went through, or the death of a spouse or child. You have grief that robs you of joy and peace of mind. If that's the pain you're carrying, I want you to know that I'm sorry you're hurting. I really am. But beyond my concern, God cares about your hurt. He sees it, and He knows all about it. You were never meant to carry that grief all on your own. Never! God says to cast all your cares upon Him, and He will care for you. Give Him your worries and troubles, and receive the gift of peace. Cast all your burdens on the Lord.

Then there are grudges—grudges also rob

us of peace. Grudges cause us to be resentful. We feel guilty when we hurt others, but we become resentful or grudging when others hurt us. You will be hurt in life, whether intentionally or unintentionally. How you respond to that hurt will determine your level of happiness in life. And for your own sake, your own peace of mind, you've got to let go of those hurts, because resentment doesn't hurt the other person; it only hurts you. You're the one who's stewing while they're living their life.

You may still be letting people from your past hurt you today, and that's not too smart. You've got to let go of your grudges. But you may say, "Rick, I can't. They hurt me too much. I can't forgive them." You're right. That's why you need Jesus Christ, because only He can give you the power to let go. Why? Because they deserve it? No, they don't deserve it; but you need to forgive for your own sake, so you can get on with your life and not stay stuck in the past over a grudge, a hurt, or a resentment. You can find peace of mind if you're willing to do the things that Christ says to do.

This Christmas You Can Find *Eternal Life*

Here are the facts of life.

First, we're all going to die someday. Now that's not a pleasant thought. I don't think you need to be morbid about it, or always be worrying about it, but the fact is we are all, each of us, going to die someday. Tomorrow, next year, ten years from now—we don't know.

Second, we're going to spend more of our life on that side of death than we're going to spend on this side. You get sixty, seventy, eighty, maybe ninety years here on this earth. But on the other side of death you'll spend the rest of eternity. Now, only a fool would go through life totally unprepared for something he knows is inevitable. It doesn't make sense to know that someday you're going to die and to not be prepared for it. Let me just say that you're not ready to live until you're ready to die. Fortunately, the good news is, that's what Christmas is all about, too. That's why God sent Jesus Christ.

> God makes us ready for heaven . . . when we put our faith and trust in Christ to save us. . . . "The man who finds life will find it through trusting God." (Rom. 1:17 TLB)

God says you can find eternal life by trusting Christ. God says, "I'll take care of your past regrets, your present problems, and your future fears." When you summarize this in one word, do you know what it's called? It's called *salvation*. And what does *salvation* mean? It means God saves me. It means Jesus saves me. It means He clears up my past, takes care of my present, and secures my future. That's one gift you'll never get anywhere else. You can't find it under the Christmas tree. You can only find it in the Man on the cross.

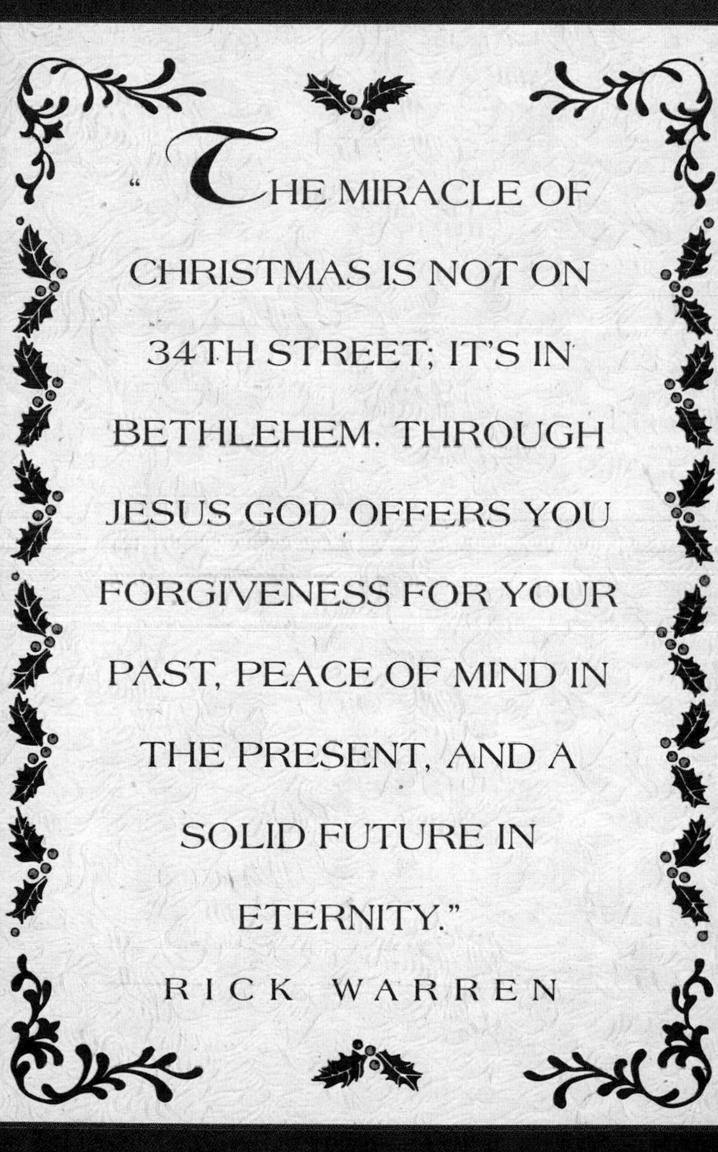
"THE MIRACLE OF
CHRISTMAS IS NOT ON
34TH STREET; IT'S IN
BETHLEHEM. THROUGH
JESUS GOD OFFERS YOU
FORGIVENESS FOR YOUR
PAST, PEACE OF MIND IN
THE PRESENT, AND A
SOLID FUTURE IN
ETERNITY."
RICK WARREN

You know what our problem is? Too often, we don't know what we're looking for in life. We think we're looking for happiness, and so we go out and we try all kinds of things to give us happiness. We think we're looking for love: "I just want somebody to love me, to fill this void in my life." Or we think we're looking for success, security, significance, or meaning and purpose in life.

We think we're looking for all these different things, but actually what we're really looking for is God. God is what you're really searching for. God is behind all those other things, and He has placed in you a God-shaped vacuum that nothing else can fill. Our hearts are restless until they find their rest in Him. But here's the good news. All the time when you were looking, and you didn't know it was God you were looking for, God was reaching out for you, too. He was working on the other end. That's why He sent Jesus Christ at Christmas so many centuries ago.

Christ, God's Son, has come to help us understand and find the true God. (1 John 5:20 TLB)

Do you see what Christmas is? Christmas is really the celebration of an invasion. It's a close encounter of the God kind. God invaded earth nearly two thousand years ago as a human being. Why? So we could know He's not some big force in the sky. He wants us to know what He's really like. The birth of His Son, Jesus, split history into A.D. and B.C. Every time you write a check, it's a reference point. Whether you're a believer or not, you're using Jesus Christ as a reference point every single day of your life: 1998, or 1999, or 2000 years from what? From the time when God sent His Son to live and die on earth.

You see, if God had wanted to communicate to cows, He would have become a cow. If God had wanted to communicate to ants, He would have become an ant. If God had wanted to communicate to dogs, He would have become a dog. But He wanted to communicate to human beings, so He became one of us, a human being. Now I can look at Jesus and say, "Oh, *that's* how God wants me to live. *That's* what God is like." By getting to know Jesus, I find out that He's not some impersonal force in the sky.

How did He come to earth? The same way all of us did: through a birth canal. Why? Because nobody is afraid of a baby. God didn't come to scare you, but to save you. So He came into the world the same way all of us did, through birth. The Bible says Jesus came to seek and to save. While you've been seeking, He's been seeking you. The miracle of Christmas is not on 34th Street; it's in Bethlehem. He says, "I offer you forgiveness for your past, peace of mind in the present, and a solid future in eternity." Those are the gifts. You say, "How do I find those gifts?" They're all wrapped up in Christ. Read this aloud: "You will seek me and find me when you seek me with all your heart" (Jer. 29:13 NIV).

Now if you don't get anything else, get this. *You matter to God.* Your problems *matter to God.* Your pain *matters to God.* Your potential *matters to God.*

God came to earth in human form, and He

is seeking you while you're seeking Him. What better time than at Christmas to make contact? He says, "Seek Me." Two thousand years ago, wise men sought Christ. And wise men still seek Christ. I challenge you to be a wise man or woman in the New Year, and to seek the Christ of Christmas, because God says, "Seek and you shall find." It's His promise. It's His gift to you.

You may be reading these words for many different reasons. Maybe you bought a book of Christmas meditations because you thought it would be a good thing for you to read on Christmas Eve. Maybe someone gave you this book as a Christmas gift. Maybe you picked it up because it was recommended to you by a friend. Whatever the reason, I want to say this: Regardless of why you are reading these words, it's not happening by accident.

Thousands of years ago, even before you were born, God knew you would be reading about Him right here, right now, at Christmastime. He brought these words to you so He could get your attention for about five minutes, so He could say to you, "I really care about you! I know everything about you. I saw your birth. I know when you're going to die. I know everything in between. I made you for a purpose, and I have a plan for your life. Life does have meaning when you get involved in My plan and develop a relationship with Me. I love you, and I want you to know Me so badly that I sent My Son to earth two thousand years ago to show you what I'm like."

What I'm talking about is not religion. I'm talking about a relationship. Religion is just man's attempt to get to God. Relationship is when you get to know Jesus Christ in a personal way and He becomes a Friend. I'm not afraid to die, because I already know what God is like.

I don't care what your background is. You may have a Catholic background, you may be a Hindu or a Buddhist, you may have a Jewish background, you may be a Protestant; maybe you have no background in religion. That doesn't matter to me. What matters is this: Have you established a personal relationship with Christ? Because those gifts—forgiveness, peace of mind, and eternal life—are wrapped up in Him.

Can you imagine being given a gift at Christmas and never unwrapping it? It would be silly. I mean, if you gave me a gift at Christmas and a year later you came over and I still hadn't unwrapped it, you'd think I was a little nutty.

"Why haven't you unwrapped it?"

"Oh, I love the wrapping paper. I'm sure I'm going to love it. I'm going to get to it one of these days."

And yet, many of you continue to move a little closer to God Christmas after Christmas after Christmas after Christmas. You've celebrated every Christmas for as many years as you are old; you know the songs and the stories, and you know what it's all about, but *you've never unwrapped the gift.*

Now what gives? What's the logic behind that? God says, "I want to offer you forgiveness, peace of mind, and eternal life," and you haven't unwrapped it? Be serious.

You're never going to be offered a greater gift than Jesus!

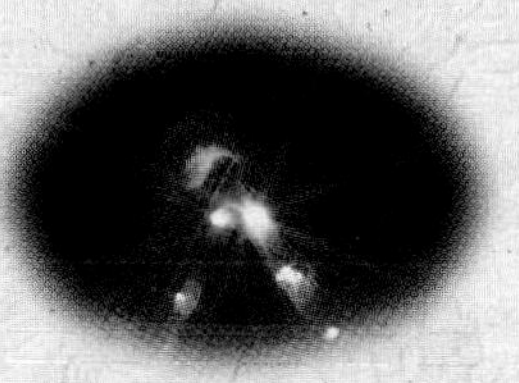

"Today your Savior was born . . . He is Christ, the Lord."

LUKE 2:11 NCV

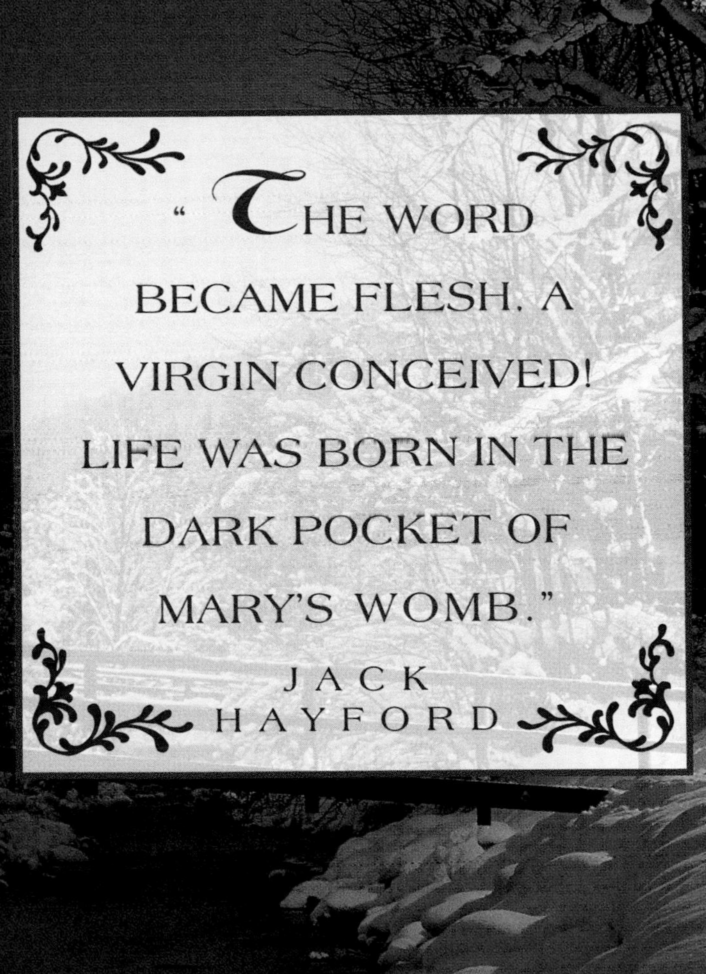
"THE WORD
BECAME FLESH. A
VIRGIN CONCEIVED!
LIFE WAS BORN IN THE
DARK POCKET OF
MARY'S WOMB."
JACK
HAYFORD

JACK HAYFORD

I Wish You A "MARY" CHRISTMAS

n the sixth month the angel Gabriel was sent from God unto a city of Galilee, named Nazareth, to a virgin espoused to a man whose name was Joseph, of the house of David; and the virgin's name was Mary. And the angel came in unto her, and said, "Hail, thou that art highly favoured, the Lord is with thee: blessed art thou among women." And when she saw him, she was troubled at his saying, and cast in her mind what manner of salutation this should be. And the angel said unto her, "Fear not, Mary: for thou hast found favour with God. And, behold, thou shalt conceive in thy womb, and bring forth a son, and shalt call his name JESUS. He shall be great, and shall be called the Son of the Highest: and the Lord God shall give unto him the throne of his father David: And he shall reign over the house of Jacob for ever; and of his kingdom there shall be no end." Then said Mary unto the angel, "How shall this be, seeing I know not a man?" And the angel answered and said

unto her, "The Holy Ghost shall come upon thee, and the power of the Highest shall overshadow thee: therefore also that holy thing which shall be born of thee shall be called the Son of God. And, behold, thy cousin Elisabeth, she hath also conceived a son in her old age: and this is the sixth month with her, who was called barren. For with God nothing shall be impossible." And Mary said, "Behold the handmaid of the Lord; be it unto me according to thy word." And the angel departed from her. (Luke 1:26–38 KJV)

I have a special Christmas greeting for you: I wish you a "Mary" Christmas. Please notice the distinction—I didn't say "Merry" Christmas. The word I used is spelled M-A-R-Y.

This Christmas, I invite you to consider the Mary Miracle. I wish it for you. In fact, I pray that the Mary Miracle will be your experience. I'm not saying, "Wouldn't it be nice." I'm asking God to provide for you what He has promised to provide. "The LORD will give grace and glory; no good thing will He withhold from those who walk uprightly" (Ps. 84:11 NKJV).

Now if we were living in another period of church history, I would hesitate to use the expression "Mary Christmas." There have been times when the walls were more pronounced between Protestantism and Catholicism. In those days it would have been tough for a Protestant minister to say, "I wish you a 'Mary' Christmas," for fear half of the congregation would rise up and say, "What's with this?"

But those walls are being broken down, and the love of God is bypassing human dogma and failure on both sides of the fences. Not just Protestant and Catholic fences—also between other denominations, families, and individuals. As the Lord moves to break down barriers between people, you find that a lot of things are redeemed, including a chance to take a fresh look at Mary and the Mary Miracle.

MARY WAS A *VIRGIN*

We need to think about the word *virgin* in view of the physical miracle that God performed. The Word became flesh. A virgin conceived! Miraculously, the seed of God entered the womb of a woman who had never been in a sexual relationship with a man. Life was born in the dark pocket of her womb, which was still sealed off by her virginity. Light and life entered, and the darkness began to breathe with life. I wish for you a "Mary" Christmas, so that in the dark pockets in your own life, there would enter today the seed of the Word of God—that Jesus would fill you, until you abound with His life.

I find the Latin word for "word" interesting. It's where we get our English word *sermon*. When a man gives a sermon, people say, "What a marvelous sermon the pastor *delivered* today." I'm fascinated that we use that term "*delivered* the sermon." When the seed of the truth of God's Word entered into a woman, the promise was, "You shall conceive and *bring forth* a son." It's the very thing that we say we want to happen. We want the life of Jesus Christ to be manifest in us. Romans 8:29 is God's target. His whole purpose for us is that we be "conformed and shaped to the likeness of Jesus." He wants there to be such a full entry of the life, truth, and Word of God—that we *deliver* Jesus. Wherever we go, we deliver the Word, the sermon, if you please. That's exactly what happened in Bethlehem two thousand years ago. The sermon was delivered. The Word was delivered—made flesh. Mary delivered a baby boy.

We need to understand the significance of Mary's virginity. Mary says, "From henceforth all generations shall call me blessed." Did she mean that every generation of people would worship her? She'd be the last person to think that. Do you see Mary at the cross? She was in the same place where we need to come. Do you see Mary in the Upper Room receiving the Holy Spirit? She received the Holy Spirit in the same way we need to receive Him. Mary's moving along on the same pathway as other believers. I think she's saying, "I'm the first one this has happened to, where into the darkness of human impossibility, the life of God entered. A pattern has been struck with me, where the life of Jesus Christ enters human flesh."

The word *blessed* means "happy." And I would say, "Mary, sweetheart, you really are happy, because it happened to you before it happened to anybody else." But she certainly isn't the last, and she doesn't summon our worship. Instead, she says, "*I want you to see the way it happened to me.*"

We tend to think of virginity only in terms of innocence and purity. Of course those terms are appropriate, but Mary's virginity did not provide an earned holiness to which God might respond with a miracle. If we think the Mary Miracle can only work in us if we are innocent, pure, and untouched, then most of us will give up and go home. I'm not talking about whether you have been tarnished or sullied in the sexual dimension. That's not the point. All of us have been marred in numerous ways by our sin and weakness. Mary's virginity is telling us this today: We don't have to be pure, innocent, or untarnished to receive the miracle.

Mary's virginity represents the impossibility, humanly speaking, of life coming forth. We need to see her virginity as a picture of the hopelessness of the situation. When we have a virgin involved, and the angelic messenger says, "You're going to bring forth a child," it's a small wonder that she says, "How can this be?"

Can you see yourself in Mary's situation? There is a dark pocket in your life, as with her womb, where life has never entered. The Mary Miracle is something that is available to each of us, but it requires an identification of the dark place, the personal poverty-pocket of your own experience, where the riches of the Lord need to enter, and where you would open up to it and say, "Okay."

The Angel Came at an Appointed *Time*

> In the sixth month the angel Gabriel was sent from God unto a city of Galilee, named Nazareth, to a virgin espoused to a man whose name was Joseph, of the house of David; and the virgin's name was Mary. (Luke 1:26–27 KJV)

The Scripture's passing reference to the sixth month may not seem very important, but please be aware of this: The Bible says, in the book of Galatians, that "in the fullness of time," God sent His Son. There was an exact time in human history that God ordained for the appearance of His Son. It's interesting to study the flow of human history, to discover all the things that converged to make this the ideal moment for the appearance of the world's Redeemer.

I used to teach a college class titled, "The Life of Christ in the Synoptic Gospels." I took two full class hours to deal with the "fullness of time." God didn't decide to send His Son on a whim or caprice, saying, "Well, maybe this is a good time." It was a part of a plan; it was precisely timed. The Bible says that at precisely the right time in human history, the angel appeared to Mary—nine months before the God-ordained appearance of the Son of God.

That "sixth month" had to do with the woman mentioned in the earlier scriptural passage. It was the sixth month of Elisabeth's pregnancy. She was not conceiving a virgin-born child, but she had been barren for a lifetime, and it was now past the time of life when she could bear children. Elisabeth had also miraculously conceived, and now she was in her sixth month. And she was to bring forth the herald of the Messiah, John the Baptist.

Just as with Mary, the Lord has a right moment for you. There is a precise moment when the Lord will approach you. There is an appointed time in which He will enter to approach the darkness of your circumstances and penetrate it with life and light. And the Bible says, "*Now* is the accepted time; *today* is the day of salvation." Jesus said, "*Today* are these words fulfilled in your ears."

The kingdom of heaven is now. It's in this moment the Lord comes. There's an appointed time, and this is it. This is when the Lord Jesus Christ enters into the human scene; He enters when we come into the God-ordained eternal presence and receive what He would have us receive.

THE ANGEL CAME TO AN APPOINTED *PLACE*

Take an imaginary journey up to a space platform with me. Now look at earth, and see it spinning there. I'm not saying that heaven is somewhere in outer space, where angels have to come sailing down and land. But I'd like for you

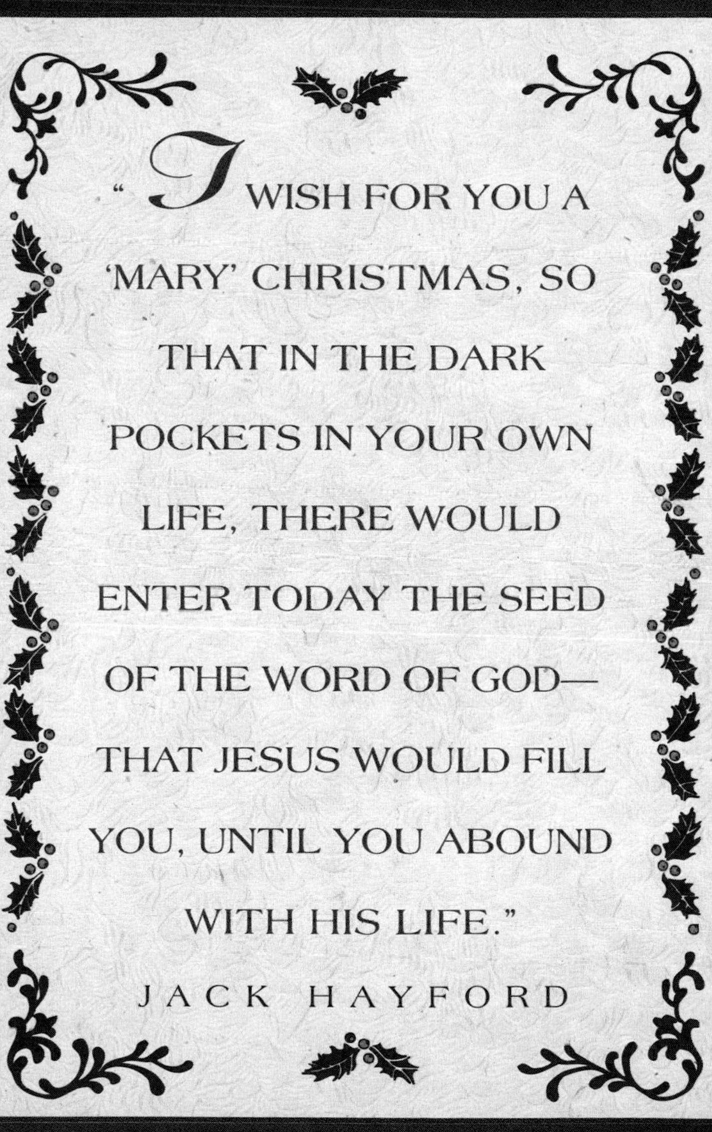

"I WISH FOR YOU A 'MARY' CHRISTMAS, SO THAT IN THE DARK POCKETS IN YOUR OWN LIFE, THERE WOULD ENTER TODAY THE SEED OF THE WORD OF GOD—THAT JESUS WOULD FILL YOU, UNTIL YOU ABOUND WITH HIS LIFE."

JACK HAYFORD

to see that spinning earth. Which continent will the message come to? Which nation? Which province? Which city? Which front porch? Which person in the house?

The angel came to Mary, a specific woman, in a specific place, Nazareth. I want to encourage you—the Lord knows your address: where you are geographically, emotionally, spiritually, financially. He knows every detail of your life. If the Father knows when a sparrow falls, don't you think He's aware of where you are, what your need is, and what your concern is? Rest in that.

THE ANGEL CAME TO AN APPOINTED *PERSON*

Your name is on the lips of God. Somehow a strange thing has happened. I believe that the miracles of modern electronics and technological advances have taught us to place more trust in man's technology than in the love and the personal attention of God. Don't be deceived: You are not a file in some heavenly computer. God does not need a desktop icon to locate you. In fact, the Scripture says we're engraved on the palms of His hands. He calls His own sheep by name. He knows *your* name, just as He knew Mary's. Let's examine the Mary Miracle even more closely.

The Angel Said Mary Was "Highly Favored"

> And the angel came in unto her, and said, "Hail, thou that art highly favoured, the Lord is with thee: blessed art thou among women." (Luke 1:28 KJV)

I'm impressed with this expression, "highly favored." You know, in my study while I'm reflecting on the Word of God, occasionally (if I were in better physical condition), I would do handsprings across the ceiling. This was one of those times! I discovered that the verb translated "highly favored" is only used two times in the whole New Testament. It's used for Mary: "*Thou* art highly favored." And if that were the only use, you'd just say, "Gee, she was something special." But it's also in Ephesians 1:6, which says, "*You* are accepted in the beloved." That's the only other place in the New Testament where this term is used.

When the angel said, "Hail Mary," he wanted her attention. He wasn't saying "Hail Mary" as an expression of worship, but in the same way that you'd say, "Hello! Greetings! Now give me your attention, because I've got good news for you!"

Like Mary, you are highly favored, too. That passage in Ephesians says, "To the saints, the accepted ones in Christ Jesus . . ." You're highly accepted. *Highly accepted, highly favored.* Every single one of us. The same thing that was said of Mary is also said of us. And that brings with it the same possibilities and the same miracle presence, because the same degree of favor is present. You and I are highly favored!

Mary Was Confused and Asked, "What *Manner* of Salutation Is This?"

And when she saw him, she was troubled at his saying, and cast in her mind what manner of salutation this should be. (Luke 1:29 KJV)

This is the only place in the New Testament where the expression "what manner of salutation?" is used in this way. Mary was asking, "What country, tribe, or people did you come from?" It's like saying, "Mister, the way you talk is not from my world. This is something I'm not familiar with in my life." The message that comes to us from the Lord is a message from another world.

Often the Word of the Lord comes to us with God's promise, but because it's not of the world that we're accustomed to—a world of doubt, fear, limitation, pride, arrogance, human meanness, habit, and bondage—we say, "That all sounds good, but I don't get it." The Lord says to us, "I want to welcome you to *My* world. Won't you come on in? Miracles happen here on a regular basis." You do not have to live in the sub-miracle level. The Mary Miracle promises that the same power Mary experienced is available to work in you.

Mary Was *Troubled* by the Message

She was troubled at his saying. (Luke 1:29 KJV)

Mary's reaction here is an emotional one. That is really an intense verb. It's not just puzzled or, "I wonder what this is?" Mary was deeply disturbed. You don't have an angel standing in front of you every day of the week. She was distraught, stirred up, in turmoil. We would be, too.

Mary Tried to *Figure Out* the Message on Her Own

[She] cast in her mind. (Luke 1:29 KJV)

Casting about in the mind is an attempt at reasoning. It's probably the hurdle we trip over most often. This verb is used repeatedly in the New Testament. In fact, I would estimate it's used twenty-five times. And almost every time, it's in a situation where people can't figure things out. They're not making any headway.

This involves a basic principle, and the sooner we receive it, the sooner we'll receive the flow of God's life and light into the dark pockets of our limitations. Here's the principle: *Quit trying to figure out how it can be done!* Would to God that we would all be released from the damnable bondage to having to reason it out in our own way. By the exercises of your mind, you are not going to figure God out or help Him along.

Mary thinks, *This is beyond me*. Yes, it is. Every miracle of the Lord is beyond you. I invite you away from your mental rationalizations, away from that limiting reasoning that brings you into the corner of death. There you are in the darkness of your barren womb with nothing happening, reasoning, "How can we get something going, God?" The Lord invites you away from your mind.

You say, "Are you calling me to reject my intellectual abilities?" No, I'm not. But you must bring those intellectual resources under the control of the Spirit and the Word of God. Rather than the mind dictating, "Well, God, You're going to have to work it out this way, or I can't see how this is going to happen," a humbling comes. Several verses later, Mary says, "Behold the handmaid of the Lord; be it unto me according to thy word." You will never say that until you've figured out that God is smarter and handier with things than you are.

We need to rest, cease our mental wrestling, and be released. As long as the mind is worshiped above the Word of God, there can only be struggling, reasoning, and rationalizing. You will weary and sweat yourself into the same dead-end street where you've been a thousand times before. You must be abandoned to the Word of God and say, "Lord, I trust You. I don't see how, but I'm not going to mess with it anymore. I bring my mind under control of the word of Your Spirit." *Then* a miracle possibility will open up.

The Angel Didn't *Criticize* Mary

And the angel said unto her, "Fear not, Mary: for thou hast found favour with God." (Luke 1:30 KJV)

The Lord doesn't come smashing in on us, saying, "Now, there, you're reasoning again." Instead, He comes to us and He addresses our real problem, which is that we're afraid. We have become so acclimated to the subnormal level of life that we inherited as Adam's offspring, that whenever God comes to work, the first thing He has to do before He can unleash it on us is say, "Don't be afraid. Just take it easy. Everything's going to be all right. We're going to do a good, healthy thing." We're so well adjusted to the absence of help. We're so used to the barrenness of the darkness that when light comes, we shield our eyes and say, "Oh, it's terrible!" The Lord says, "You were made to walk in that Light and to look up into it. Don't be afraid. Don't be afraid!"

The Angel Made a *Pronouncement*

And, behold, thou shalt conceive in thy womb, and bring forth a son, and shalt call his name JESUS. He shall be great, and shall be called the Son of the Highest: and the Lord God shall give unto him the throne of his father David: And he shall reign over the house of Jacob for ever; and of his kingdom there shall be no end. (Luke 1:31–33 KJV)

I want you to notice a recurring word. The angel says, "Thou *shalt*, [thou] *shalt*, he *shall*, [he] *shall*, the Lord God *shall*, he *shall*, there *shall*." *Angel* means "messenger." I'm not an angel from heaven, but I'm an angel sent from God, and I come to give you these glad tidings: *The Lord's life* shall *enter into your circumstances*. There shall be His triumph, His health, His fullness, His provisions.

Mary Wondered, "How *Shall This Be*?"

Then said Mary unto the angel, "How shall this be, seeing I know not a man?" (Luke 1:34 KJV)

Mary says the most understandable and forgivable thing that anybody could possibly say in that situation. She says, "You're talking about life, the birth of a child." You and I would say, "You're talking about Jesus coming forth in me in the dark pocket of my own need, crisis, and past." What she's essentially saying is, "I haven't had the relationship that will bring this about." Or, "I haven't had the experience necessary for this."

You may have thought or said, "Some people have the kind of relationship with God in which they can believe anything, but I don't have that kind of great faith." If the Lord were approaching us on the grounds of our experience, relationship, or what people can do, then there would be no miracle possibility—everything tainted by human flesh is destined for death. He doesn't approach Mary and say, "Now, you're going to marry Joseph, and when that child comes, it will become the Son of God somehow. It will be just a normal human, sanctified by God."

The Lord's not inviting you to work your way through things so He can bless them. His miracle is not going to be based on your experience, growth or development, effort, or what you can produce at your level. It's not based on your relationship. It's based on His promise and commitment. It's based on His declaration.

There entered into that young woman, into the sealed-off, dark pocket of that womb, the seed of the living God. There was a miracle entry of God's life. How? I don't know. But the God who begat life from nothing, who breathed into that clay the breath of life, is a God fully capable of creating life within the womb of that virgin. The God who made you for better things than you may have experienced is fully able to fulfill His destined purpose for you by just the touch of His breath upon you.

THE ANGEL EXPLAINED THAT IT WOULD HAPPEN THROUGH THE *HOLY SPIRIT*

And the angel answered and said unto her, "The Holy Ghost shall come upon thee, and the power of the Highest shall overshadow thee." (Luke 1:35 KJV)

In other words Mary was told, "You're going to be enveloped in the glory of God, lady. The glory of the Lord is going to come over you."

It's worthwhile to note that Mary was probably no more than fifteen or sixteen years old. That was a very marriageable age in those days. And in her mental reasoning, I think there's a message for us. Clearly, Mary wasn't stupid, but she was in a society that didn't have the advantage of our educational processes. Here's someone who holds the lesser advantage in terms of gender—she didn't have the privileged position in the culture, because she was a woman. And she was young. Not just inexperienced in terms of marriage or sex, Mary was inexperienced with life.

If she had been a Solomon-type person stroking his gray beard and saying, "How shall this be?" I think we could understand a little bit. The old man would have had some experience. I'm not mocking her teenage point of view, but it's almost laughable that someone so inexperienced is saying, "I can't figure this out." Of course you can't! And, young or old, we all need to take that position. Don't put any trust in the accumulated wisdom of your years, because your experience, wisdom, and knowledge don't matter. God's going to work it out by the ministry of the Holy Spirit.

The Angel Spoke About Other *Miracles* Happening Around Mary

Therefore also that holy thing which shall be born of thee shall be called the Son of God. And, behold, thy cousin Elisabeth, she hath also conceived a son in her old age: and this is the sixth month with her, who was called barren. (Luke 1:35–36 KJV)

I think it's especially lovely that the angel tells Mary, "I know it's hard for you to believe this miracle is going to happen in you. But there are miracles happening around you. Consider Elisabeth, your cousin, with her miracle." Now it's different with Elisabeth, because her son John wasn't a virgin-born child. But he was still a miracle. Elisabeth was past childbearing age.

Ever feel like saying, "I can't even *conceive* of

that happening in me"? That's an interesting use of words, isn't it? Look around, because there are other people in whom the Holy Spirit is working miracles. There's nothing wrong with recognizing that the actions of God are already going on in somebody else.

The Angel Assured Mary That Nothing Is *Impossible* with God

For with God nothing shall be impossible. (Luke 1:37 KJV)

I rarely point out passages of Scripture in which there is an omission in the translation. To begin with, there aren't very many places where that happens. Also, sometimes people get too nervous about their translations, and I don't think you need to be. But here there is a word that should have been translated another way.

Almost every commentary acknowledges it. The word that's translated "thing" should be translated "word." "Thing" refers to the spoken word of God.

When God speaks His word, the word *rama* is used. So it's saying here, "For with God, no word shall be without power." Consider how the Amplified Bible translates this: "For with God nothing is ever impossible and no word from God shall be without power or impossible of fulfillment." The Oxford translation is beautiful: "For no word of God is without power." With God, any word is attended with power to see that it's executed. When God speaks His word, He commissions the ministry of the Holy Spirit to perform it. God will hasten His word to perform it.

When the Lord makes a commitment to you or me, we can know that it is not just so many verbs, adjectives, and nouns tumbling out of His lips. He's not saying, "Here's something you can hang on and play with for a while." His word comes with the attendant ministry of the Holy Spirit to make it work.

This miracle of life in the dark womb of this virgin girl is not the first or only time God has moved in the darkness. In creation we see Him doing the same thing: In the midst of chaos and confusion, His word brings life. Into the darkness of slavery in Egypt, God worked out deliverance. In the darkness of this present world, the Son of Righteousness is going to come and take His church. The Lord will come and meet you in the darkness of your situation, and He will work His glory there.

MARY OPENED HERSELF TO THE *POSSIBILITIES*

And Mary said, "Behold the handmaid of the Lord; be it unto me according to thy word." And the angel departed from her. (Luke 1:37 KJV)

Mary's openness to the working of the Lord is the basic principle that will work the Mary

Miracle in us. So yes, I wish you a "Mary" Christmas: I pray that in the sealed-off, dark pocket of need in your life, you would say, "Okay, I receive the entrance of the word that gives life and light. Let there come forth the Son of God in His full power in me."

What is it that your heart hungers for?

What is your need?

What is the stress point in your life?

Where is the darkness?

Where's the shadow?

James 1:17 says, "Every good gift and every perfect gift . . . comes down from the Father of lights, with whom there is no variation or shadow of turning." The Lord would say He is the Father of light in your darkness. That's the good gift He offers: The light of the world has entered the dark pocket of your own need, the womb of your circumstances, sealed off to possibilities. With God nothing shall be impossible, and He'll move in right where you are.

Wherever you are, whatever you lack, wherever His light must enter to release and bring health, strength, wisdom, discretion, and understanding, I say to you, in the name of Jesus: "Mary" Christmas is what you need. I wish you a Mary Christmas.

"For with God nothing

shall be impossible."

LUKE 1:37 KJV